Toward an African Christianity

Inculturation Applied

Eugene Hillman, C.S.Sp.

Paulist Press
New York and Mahwah, N.J.

Library of Congress Cataloging-in-Publication Data

Hillman, Eugene.
    Toward an African Christianity : inculturation applied / Eugene Hillman.
        p. cm.
    Includes bibliographical references and index.
    ISBN 0-8091-3381-4 (pbk.)
    1. Catholic Church—Africa, Sub-Saharan. 2. Christianity and culture. 3. Maasai (African people)—Religion. 4. Africa, Sub-Saharan—Church history. 5. Kenya—Religion. 6. Tanzania—Religion. I. Title.
BX1680.3.H55   1993
261'.0967—dc20   92-39526
                                                                              CIP

Published by Paulist Press
997 Macarthur Boulevard
Mahwah, New Jersey 07430

Printed and bound in the United States of America

Contents

87205

Acknowledgments

The production of this book was made possible by the help given me in a variety of ways by many different people. In the very first place an expression of gratitude is due to the Maasai people among whom I lived for many years in both Kenya and Tanzania. They provided me with the human support required for missionary work in an alien cultural world. Their ways of being human and religious presented me with the anthropological and theological questions I have been wrestling with since my arrival among them in 1951. A public expression of gratitude is due also to Bishop Colin Davies of Ngong Diocese in Kenya. Although sometimes hesitant, his patience with my efforts to think critically about the conventional methods of most missionaries was more important to me than he realized. Among my fellow workers in the African bush, special mention is due to Edward Kelly and Vincent Donovan.

Among my academic colleagues I am most grateful to the following theologians for their critical reading of earlier drafts of this book, and for their helpful comments: Roger Haight of Weston School of Theology in Cambridge, William M. Thompson and Michael Slusser of Duquesne University in Pittsburgh. To Francis Malinowski, also of Duquesne University's theology department, a very special word of thanks is due. With extraordinary patience, he came to my rescue whenever I got lost in the dense forest of Word Perfect processing.

...You may and you must have an African Christianity. Indeed, you possess the human values and characteristic forms of culture...capable of a richness all its own, and genuinely African. You have the strength and the grace necessary for this...because you are Christians and you are Africans.

> Pope Paul VI, to bishops
> at All-Africa Symposium
> in Uganda (1969)

The term "inculturation" may be a neologism, but it expresses very well one factor of the great mystery of the Incarnation.

> Pope John Paul II,
> *Catechesi tradende,* no.
> 53 (1979)

Introduction

The idea that the divine Word became a human being, like the rest of us in everything except sin, is Christianity's central and most astonishing religious symbol. It is also a source of scandal among Christians who have always found its elementary implications difficult to apply in the concrete situations of everyday life. God, in whose image we are created, is united forever with everyone who comes into the world, making "each one a sharer in Jesus Christ," as Pope John Paul II expressed it in his first encyclical letter.[1] But many Christians fail persistently to act upon the belief that the Lord is truly present in the least, the lost and the left-out among us. It is even more difficult to love our enemies in whom also we are supposed to acknowledge the divine presence. Yet, for the salvation of Christians, these implications are the finally decisive issues. They are mandatory principles of action flowing directly from the good news communicated to us in Jesus of Nazareth: that the divine Spirit is among us always and everywhere present in each human being.

The particular consequence of the incarnation addressed in the following pages is also a rock of scandal to many. This implication, indicating the appropriate posture of the church vis-à-vis humankind's irreducible cultural diversity, is often called the missionary principle of "contextualization" or "indigenization." This is an action-principle governing the way in which the Christian faith is supposed to be at home in the diverse cultural worlds of the varied peoples making up the whole of God's beloved humanity. In this regard the Second Vatican Council (1963-65) spoke of incarnating the Christian faith among the nations. So it is a basic assumption of the reflections offered in this book that the incarnation of the divine Word is paradigmatic for the life and activity of the church. What was done once and for all in Jesus of Nazareth at a moment in the history of one particular people is a model for what is supposed to happen through the church among each people in the course of humankind's ongoing history.

The arguments supporting this outward–looking ecclesiology are presented here against the background of missionary activity in Africa, and in the theological terms of the Catholic tradition, as reflected notably in the writings of Karl Rahner and Bernard Lonergan. With the appropriate changes, however, these arguments are relevant to the situation of Christians anywhere in the countries of the south, and they speak to all who are engaged in cross-cultural ministries, especially where the otherness of others is respected, and people are encouraged to be themselves while being Christians. According to the teaching of Vatican II, the church is supposed to become present among all these peoples "in the same way that Christ by his incarnation committed himself to the particular social and cultural circumstances of the people among whom he lived."[2] In other words, through a "wonderful exchange," and "in keeping with the economy of the incarnation (*ad intsar oeconomiae incarnationis*)," the Christian community is supposed to "transform and assimilate into itself" all the cultural "riches of the nations."[3]

Catholics, more than other Christians, use the classical theological term, "incarnation," analogically. The incarnation of the divine Word in Jesus of Nazareth necessarily entails the full acceptance of an historically conditioned culture, because no human being exists outside of a specific historico-cultural context. In becoming Christians, therefore, far from stepping out of their real-life situations, the peoples of the world are expected to be fully themselves in their respective historical contexts, and to enrich the universal Christian community with their particular cultural patrimonies. This analogical understanding gained wide currency just after the Second World War, especially in France through the 1947 pastoral letter of the Archbishop of Paris, Cardinal Suhard, who saw the incarnation as "the essential law of the apostolate." This usage appears again in the writings of Pope Paul VI and Pope John Paul II; also in the statement of the Vatican's International Theological Commission on "Faith and Inculturation."[4]

There is now a growing tendency to designate the principle of incarnation by the neologism "inculturation," and to use both terms interchangeably. As with the other principles derived from belief in the incarnation, and despite much eloquent lip service, there has always been formidable resistance to any attempts to enflesh the faith in non-European cultural ways of

being human and religious. Hence the urgency of the principle of inculturation understood as the church's effort to communicate the message of Christ
by incarnating it in the lives and cultures of each people, thereby enabling
them "to bring forth from their own living traditions original expressions of
Christian life, celebration and thought."[5] "At least in theory," observes Karl
Rahner, "the inculturation of Christianity into the different cultures is everywhere admitted as a duty of the Church."[6]

This "duty of the Church," because it raises hard questions and
involves unprecedented challenges, is both difficult and urgent. "It is difficult," says Walter Brueggemann, "because we have become so accustomed
to our Euro-American domination that alternative expressions of Christian
faith are discomforting and odd." Nevertheless, some positive action in this
regard is urgently needed, "because our cultural domination is now ending,
and we dare not any longer confuse our cultural domination with the powers
and claims of the gospel, which may indeed be embedded in many cultural
forms."[7] So, geopolitical considerations may be a spur to action where theological reflection has yielded only erudite papers on the topic.

The four chapters of the present volume may be counted among the
erudite papers. But they are, in the first instance, a direct result of the twenty-
five years of my life given to the service of the church's missionary outreach
in East Africa just south of the equator. So I have some firsthand experience
of what has been going on under the banner of Christianity in these parts;
also some share in the failures of this enterprise, which I have written about
critically. Although the principle of incarnation was hardly mentioned, much
less applied, during that quarter of a century, vast numbers of Africans were
persuaded to enter the church.

Was this unprecedented church growth a consequence of the gospel of
Jesus received and understood? Or was it merely an element in the colonial
process of westernization, promoting a foreign religion together with all the
other exports from Europe: western clothing, schooling, music, languages,
technologies, economies, ideologies and weapons? Absent any serious
efforts to incarnate the Christian faith in African cultural worlds, and considering the generally negative attitude of most missionaries toward the "pagan"
ways of Africans, it may be assumed that what passed for evangelism during
the past hundred years was in reality a dissemination of the western experiences and expressions of Christian faith. These foreign religious interpretations of the faith, with their alien cultural accoutrements and social constructions, were translated literally into African cultural worlds. Typically, the
translations were exclusively linguistic and literalistic. In some countries it
was considered sufficient to use only a regional *lingua franca.* A case in

point is the Christian use of the Swahili language as the principal system for communicating with more than a hundred distinctive ethnic-culture groups, each with its own language, in Tanzania and parts of Kenya.

"What matters is to evangelize cultures," as Pope Paul VI said in *Evangelii nuntiandi*. But this has not been done in Africa where now, as in many other places, "the split between the Gospel and cultures is the tragedy of our time."[8] Without prejudice to the good intentions and generous efforts of countless church workers, it is widely recognized today that the persistent ethnocentrism of missionaries and their sending congregations has marked Christianity as something foreign and extrinsic to Africa. It has the appearance of an imported shirt that can be readily slipped on or off as the occasion requires.

Nevertheless, all the mistakes in cross-cultural communication, making evangelization so problematical, did not entirely preclude the possibility of the Christian message getting through to many people. After all, God's grace is more powerful than our obtuseness. So the large numbers of African Christians, both nominal and authentic, are highly significant for the future of the church on our planet. Within a decade, if not sooner, there will be more Christians in Africa than there are in North America, where the population's median age is more than twice that of Africa. We may expect, therefore, that the shepherds from Africa at the next general meeting of the Christian World Church will be numerically commensurate with the size of their flocks. We may hope that, in collaboration with their colleagues from the other countries of the south, they will move Christianity away from its Euro-American monocentrism, and toward an authentically catholic pluricentrism. They could, if they wish, start the process now. After all, God's creation is gloriously pluriform, and each galaxy in the universe is a center. On what grounds, then, do ecclesiastical office holders continue to act as though God wills the expressions and celebrations of African Christians to remain essentially, as they are now, Euro-centric reproductions of the historically and culturally conditioned religious experience of western peoples?

It is understandable that many African church leaders, conscientious in their duty to safeguard the integrity of Christian doctrine, should be reluctant to move in the direction indicated by the principle of incarnation in Africa's countless cultural worlds which previously, in the name of Christ, they had been taught to ignore, and sometimes even to condemn. It is yet to be appreciated widely that the church's chronic monoculturalism poses a greater threat than pluralism to the catholicity of Christianity and to the integrity of its teachings. Calls for the application of the principle of inculturation are not demands for the introduction of beliefs contrary to Christian faith.

Manifold pluralism is required precisely for the sake of intelligible communication in the terms of humankind's myriad sociocultural, linguistic, artistic and common sense differences. "The stranger acts strangely," says Bernard Lonergan, "because his common sense is not our own." Christian doctrine is properly communicated not only through the linguistic symbol systems of each people in their respective times and places, but also through their own "rituals, narratives, titles, parables, metaphors, modes of praise and blame, of command and prohibition, of promise and threat."⁹ Without these culturally invented symbol systems, there can be no adequate communication of Christian doctrine.

Without trying to comment on everything that seems problematical, the first chapter describes under selected headings some consequences of the dominant missionary-pastoral methods and ecclesiastical structures employed in sub-Saharan Africa during the modern missionary period from the late nineteenth century to the present. The second chapter is a summary statement of the radical missionary and pastoral thinking officially introduced by, most notably, the Second Vatican Council and by elements within the World Council of Churches, vis-à-vis the modern discovery that humankind's multi-cultural condition is compatible with the teachings of Jesus. The third chapter is a positive appreciation of the major themes and rites of one particular African traditional religion—that of the Maasai people of Kenya and Tanzania—which, with the help of contemporary theologians, may be seen as a culturally appropriate instrument of God's saving grace. The fourth chapter is a tentative effort to suggest how and to what extent, in virtue of the principle of inculturation, that particular African religion might serve as the local Christian community's religious system transformed by their faith in Christ.

The principle of inculturation has also some far-reaching implications for Christians living within the cultural zones of Europe and North America where western cultures have been undergoing profound and rapid changes during the decades following the Second World War. Now that monarchical and dictatorial styles of governance have become obsolete and odious among the peoples everywhere in the world, it is surely time to examine church structures with a view to reducing authoritarian paternalism, and maximizing respect for the workings of the Holy Spirit among the ordinary faithful. Nor is it any longer credible for church functionaries to answer complex moral questions simply by quoting ancient authors who could not have imagined, much less addressed, these questions as they have arisen in later historical periods and in different cultural contexts.

Another large question treated only tangentially in this book—because it arises only where inculturation has already occurred—is the extent to which the embodiment of the Christian faith in the forms and structures of a particular cultural world may have the effect of burying, under heaps of cultural accretions, the central message of Jesus. Some would argue that this has happened in the modern western world where the message is hard to find among the layers of utilitarian individualism, techno-economic rationality, systemic greed, tribalism and pious posturing. Bishop Lesslie Newbigin suggests that this culture of western modernity may be, more than almost any other culture in the world, resistant to the gospel[10]—even as many people caught in its web try passionately to imagine themselves more "saved" than all the others.

So, there is much more to be said about the implications of the incarnation. For this reason, the reflections offered in the present volume should be of interest not only to people concerned with cross-cultural ministries, but also to all contemporary students of Christian theology, including those who are perplexed by the symbolic meaning of the incarnation.

1

The Colonial Model Persisting

In so far as one preaches the gospel as it has been developed within one's own culture, one is preaching not only the gospel but also one's own culture. In so far as one is preaching one's own culture, one is asking others not only to accept the gospel but also to renounce their own culture and accept one's own.

—Bernard Lonergan [1]

During five centuries of colonialism, western Europeans gained and maintained control over most of the lands and peoples of the southern hemisphere. The north's political, economic and cultural hegemony was accomplished through a variety of nefarious means. In Latin America it was done through a combination of pillaging, slaughtering and enslaving vast populations. Similar iniquities characterized the "scramble for Africa" in the nineteenth and twentieth centuries.[2] In immense regions south of the Sahara, European domination was gradually consolidated by dispossessing the peoples of their best agricultural land, pasturage and natural resources; also by reducing large populations to pools of cheap labor for the plantations of colonial settlers and foreign companies.[3]

Where climates were too harsh for European settlers, as in the western Sahel countries, the indigenous people were forced to produce cash crops for the export market (e.g., groundnuts, cotton). There was little regard for the consequent environmental degradation, and less for the fair compensation of the primary producers. By giving priority to the interests of agribusiness, while neglecting the production and storage of food crops needed by Africa's own growing populations, the way was prepared for the subsequent famines recurring periodically in some sub-Saharan countries. "Overpopulation" is the facile term commonly used to blame the victims themselves for these epidemics of starvation resulting from land-use policies inspired by greed.

When not deliberately trying to destroy them, the colonial processes invariably undermined the systems, values and views of entire cultural worlds. The victims were most effectively disarmed by varied and persistent assaults against their cultures. Stripped naked and taught, in schools and churches, to be ashamed of themselves, their "primitive" and "pagan" ways, the people were coerced, morally as well as physically, into clothing them-selves with the ways of the invading cultures. The colonial incursions, although they brought literacy and antibiotics, made westernization the way of human "advancement." Many people came to believe that "progress" con-sists not in being themselves, but in imitating foreign ways. Authentic human development was thus radically misconceived, hence extensively precluded. Wittingly or not, Christian missionaries from Europe and North America—even if their motives were higher than those of the soldiers, administrators, merchants and settlers of colonialism—were accomplices to these crimes.

Religious activity, aimed at displacing Africa's traditional religious symbol systems, and replacing them with foreign imports, was the greatest threat to the survival of African cultures. This is so, because these cultures are intimately bound up with the people's traditional religious experiences, perceptions and articulations. Moreover, the establishment of Christian con-gregations among the "natives" lent an aura of respectability and a cloak of legitimacy to the morally reprehensible enterprise of colonialism.

The institutional constructions holding together any society are always in need of legitimations which "explain" to the members, and "justify" to them, what is going on. Such "explanations" and "justifications" need to be contrived in situations of colonial domination. A plausible story, rationaliz-ing vast inequalities, gross injustices and patent absurdities, is worked into the socialization process. So it is that subsequent generations usually contin-ue uncritically to support the expanding institutional order. The story—in this case, the myth of "progress" or "advancement" over the "primitive" and "pagan" ways of traditional Africans—becomes what Peter Berger and Thomas Luckmann call "a canopy of legitimations, stretching over the soci-ety a cover of both cognitive and normative interpretations."[4]

The Berger-Luckmann analysis of socialization enables us to appreciate what happened to many African peoples under the resocializing processes of colonialism. Their description of the processes helps us to understand what became of so many of Africa's traditional cultural systems, worldviews, values and self-images under the impact of the social, economic and religious institutions introduced during the colonial period. As part of their social control system, the foreigners' definitions of situations (social, economic, political, religious, ethical, artistic) were imposed and maintained in fairly official tones. In due course these impositions were painstakingly institutionalized, lest the indigenous systems, values and views of the colonized populations reassert themselves "seditiously" in the form of challenges, redefinitions, or even as pointed questions. In the words of Berger and Luckmann:

> The children must be "taught to behave" and, once taught, must be "kept in line."...The more conduct is institutionalized, the more predictable and thus the more controlled it becomes. If socialization into the institutions has been effective, outright coercive measures can be applied economically and selectively. Most of the time conduct will occur "spontaneously" within the institutionally set channels. The more, on the level of meaning, conduct is taken for granted, the more possible alternatives to the institutional "programmes" will recede, and the more predictable and controlled conduct will be.[5]

While the resocializing forces of the colonial invaders were thus striving to recondition and "keep in line" hundreds of diverse African populations, the traditional institutions of these peoples served as defensive bunkers for indigenous cultural values and social structures. When spears and arrows failed against rifles and the Maxim gun, some political, cultural and economic accommodations were made. But the indigenous symbol systems, such as the major rites of passage and the local religious celebrations, served powerfully to sustain the integrity of the besieged communities.

The social identity, cohesion and continuity of any community depends upon the strength of its symbol systems. These systems contain and communicate a society's common meanings, values, perceptions, judgments, goals and worldview. Without these commonalities communities gradually fall apart. Populations, thus divided, then become progressively more vulnerable to foreign manipulators and to the emerging selfish individualism of their own members. In this regard, some African cultures have proven more durable than others, but all have suffered significant erosion during the past one hundred years. Thoroughly conditioned by the institutions introduced under colonialism, some African leaders work today, even more zealously than their former colonial bosses, for the suppression of traditional African ways of being human and religious. Some Christians, confusing Euro-American cultural forms and practices with the good news of Jesus Christ, are unable to even imagine how any African religious forms and practices might be compatible with Christianity, much less how they could be signs and instruments of saving faith.

Because of their current historical understanding of such social processes in the present post-colonial period, many people in the politically "independent" countries of Africa are critically reevaluating the results of colonialism. Increasing numbers of African church leaders, and many Christians engaged in cross-cultural ministries, are now asking searching questions about the religious, ethical and evangelical authenticity of what has been going on. Was the whole process of evangelization in sub-Saharan Africa deeply flawed from the beginning by colonial assumptions, attitudes and methods? Viewing the scene from ground level in these lands inhabited by some of the world's poorest populations, one wonders whether or to what extent the church's foreign structures and institutions—symbolized in many areas by mountains of paraphernalia imported from the north, including the splendid residences of bishops, archbishops and apostolic nuncios—are resting on foundations of sand?

Thanks to the increasing influence of the social sciences during the twentieth century, together with the decline of colonialism and the modifications of imperialism since the end of the Second World War, the mainline Christian churches are now trying to transcend their congenital and chronic Euro-American ethnocentrism. This much is evident from the writings of contemporary theologians, ethicists and missiologists; also from the official pastoral and missionary directives issued periodically by various church bodies and high level functionaries. The Roman Catholic articulation of this entirely new orientation toward an authentic cultural pluralism in the churches of the non-western world—actually recognizing the rights of all peoples to their own indigenous ways of being human and religious—is documented in the chapter following this one. In the present chapter the focus of attention is on the present image and practice of Christianity among the more than eight hundred distinctive ethnic-culture groups of people living in Africa south of the Sahara.

In spite of the rhetoric of incarnation, inculturation, indigenization and contextualization, the general scene is characterized by little more than literal translations, cautious adaptations and questionable substitutions. Full-blood-ed incarnations of Christianity, if they exist anywhere in Africa, are well hidden. Instead, there is in most Christian congregations an uneasy clinging to the model of missionary and pastoral ministry developed during the colonial period under the influence of a colossal western cultural arrogance. The paternalism of this model is now expressed more gently, however, and it is animated, as in the past, by the extraordinary generosity of missionaries and pastors. The dominant method used, therefore, in making Christianity palpably present in the several parts of Africa with which I am familiar, is still the importation of strictly western suppositions, systems, institutions, structures, symbols, myths, rules, concepts, practices, customs and costumes.

These foreign elements impact heavily upon the local cultures, ignoring, if not completely undermining, traditional worldviews, art forms, customary laws, ethical norms and immemorial practices. Indeed, in the usual missionary and pastoral approach of both Catholics and Protestants, African peoples have often been treated as though they were merely aggregates of spiritual nomads. There is still a persistent tendency to perceive these individual "souls" in abstraction not only from their physical bodies, but also from the cultural matrices in which they were socialized as persons of a particular time and place.

Now, after one hundred years of the colonial model of missionary work in their country, the Catholic bishops of Zambia are urging their people to take up the challenge of inculturation. These church leaders have recognized officially that the early missionaries in Africa, as "people of their own time, culture and mentality...may not have been sufficiently sensitive to some positive aspects of our traditions."[6] In language less diplomatic, the same lack of cultural sensitivity is noted by an African theologian. In the view of Eboussi Boulaga of Cameroon, African Christians have been suffering, up to now, under "a Christianity of empire." This "imposes itself only by tearing up its converts by the roots, out of where-they-live, out of their being-in-the-world, presenting them with the faith only at the price of depriving them of their capacity to generate the material and spiritual conditions of their existence."[7] So, Africans are still seen as "good Christians" to the extent that they are able to approximate all the cultural ways and religious practices introduced by the early missionaries from Europe or North America.

"CHRISTIAN" NAMES

This systematic detachment of people from their roots in the real world has been fostered in a variety of ways; indeed, in a thousand different ways, both blatant and subtle. The alien and alienating character of Christianity in Africa is still being flaunted, for example, by the widespread practice of imposing foreign names (mostly Jewish or European) at baptism. The people are told that, according to church law, only the names of officially recognized saints may be used. This narrowly juridical interpretation, oblivious of the long-standing contrary practice in some countries of the north, does not attend to the basic question of how, in the first place, any name ever became recognized as a saint's name. It even ignores, on this point, the cautious flexibility reflected in the revised code of canon law, promulgated in 1983. In many African parishes, therefore, the use of authentically African names at baptism is precluded. This happens even where traditional names have important social significance. In some places, this insistence upon foreign names comes up against deeply rooted and profoundly meaningful ways of choosing the names of children.

Even today, in spite of all the lip-service given to the recognition of cultural pluralism, only a minority of missionaries and pastors are inclined to encourage the use of African names at baptism. In territories where the first missionaries were Irish, the name "Patrick" still proliferates. Where they were Italians, people are still being baptized with such names as "Pasquale." Names like "Wolfgang" are still found in areas served originally by German missionaries. Protestant communities are no less foreign in their "Christian" symbols. Those from England and North America, for example, promote names such as "Jackson," "Livingstone" and "Duncan." Such westernizing symbolism suggests the active presence of either a perduring ignorance of, or an implicit contempt for, African traditions.

One may wonder whether, in the days of the early missionaries in Africa, the use of such symbols may have been part of a much larger game aimed at turning Africans into consumers of western produce, including the multiple brands of Christianity invented in Europe and North America. We may recall Dr. David Livingstone's famous remark about the commercial implications of converting millions of Africans to a type of Christianity clothed with the manufactures of Manchester's textile industries. Is there some connection between this pious commercialism and modernity's culture of the market urging people to define themselves not by their ethnicity and their traditional cultural values, but in terms of the manufactured things they possess abundantly and the goods they consume conspicuously?

But why make an issue of the use of foreign names? Surely this custom is just one of the numerous peripheral practices carried over from Judaism; it hardly touches the heart of Christianity. Besides, as the usual argument goes, the use of the same names everywhere in the world signifies the unity of all

Christians and their continuity with the officially recognized saints in heaven. Unity or uniformity? For hundreds of years, right into the third quarter of the twentieth century, a similar rationale was offered by ecclesiastical officialdom for retaining the Latin language not only in the liturgy but also as the medium of theological education in Catholic seminaries. There is an interesting parallel in the Islamic custom of generally using Arabic names, language, prayer forms, customs and laws.

Mindless ethnocentrism? Arrogant monoculturalism? Both, obviously. But the psychosocial implications are far-reaching. It is no wonder that Muslims who are not Arabs, and Christians who are not Euro-Americans are now challenging these vestiges of religious imperialism.

KIKUYU NAMES

In a doctoral dissertation at Belgium's Louvain University, an African scholar, guided by the norms and directives of the Second Vatican Council, proposed several important issues to be faced by African Christians concerned with "salvaging the local missionary church from a rootless Christianity based and vested in foreign cultural values."[8] The naming practices of Kenya's Kikuyu people, in tension with some pastors reluctant to abandon this Europeanizing symbolism of "Christian" names, is just one of many similar issues.

The names of all the newborn members of Kikuyu society are predetermined according to a comprehensive scheme designed to do what it signifies. The traditional system of names points to and helps to establish the people's powerful and pervasive sense of belonging to one another in the unity of family, clan, ethnicity and culture. The names also bespeak mutual responsibilities. The firstborn son is given the name of his paternal grandfather whose memory is thus perpetuated generation after generation. The second son has the name of his maternal grandfather, while the third boy perpetuates the name of his own father's eldest brother. The fourth male child is named after his mother's first brother. The fifth son gets the name of his father's second brother, and the sixth boy continues the name of his mother's second brother.

An exactly parallel scheme is used for relating each daughter to a paternal or maternal relative whose memory is to be perpetuated. So, in this patrilineal society the name to be continued by the first daughter is that of her father's mother. The second daughter is named after her mother's mother. Following the same sequential pattern used for the sons, the remaining daughters are named after their respective paternal and maternal aunts. Nor is this just a matter of perpetuating the names of relatives who become eventually, through the memory of subsequent generations, the "living-dead."

This naming system binds together people of different generations, families and clans; it creates mutual duties that are lifelong and supportive. Beyond the relationships of the nuclear family, each child has also a unique connection with another person in the extended family. The one whose name is perpetuated in the child is expected to be for that child a model human being, a caring friend and educator. In due course, the child is expected to reciprocate, as persons are supposed to do in such relationships, in accord with their own cultural self-understanding and in response to the exigencies of the human condition.

Given the cultural significance of this immemorial practice of the Kikuyu people, tensions are inevitable between traditional-minded parishioners and pastors who interpret church law too narrowly. In such cases a sympathetic pastor sometimes compromises by allowing an African name to be given together with a Jewish or European one. But the foreign name is entered in the baptismal register as the official "Christian" name, although the African name is the one more likely to be used during the life of this new Christian.

Such legalistic restraints serve, in effect, to discourage the use of traditional African names, as most people try to avoid arguments with their pastors. This is especially so when the pastors themselves, having been fully resocialized into western ways during their years of seminary training, imagine that "progress" or modernity is a matter of imitating the ways of the west, and that African customs are to be scorned as "pagan" and "primitive." But there is also a more serious assumption here, tacit, unexamined and erroneous; it is that, before the advent of white preachers from abroad, the Holy Spirit was not always and everywhere sanctifying people bearing traditional African names.

The Kikuyu case illustrates the wisdom of giving traditional names to the newly arrived members of many ethnic-culture groups in Africa. Among other meanings, which outsiders have hardly begun to fathom, African naming ceremonies may symbolize the flesh and blood continuity and identity of a whole ethnic community. For many different peoples in the non-western world a name is much more than a legal label for distinguishing individuals one from another. "A name is a weighty word," writes Harvard University's historian of religion, Lawrence E. Sullivan: "it is a statement of one's specific presence in the world....Receiving a name, capturing the sound-name of another...and knowing others by name, molds the person's entire being in the shape of a sound."[9]

The conferring and celebrating of indigenous names, as initiation rites, provide the recipients, and indeed all the participants, with a fresh awareness of their historicity and cultural embeddedness. Such customs teach individuals that they are not merely biological products, but cultural creations within a social process enabling them, with the help of a specific context of relationships, to become fully human. "The meaning of names and the naming process," says Professor Sullivan, "help compose the significant order of society...."[10] Through meaningful cultural practices and their historical transmission to subsequent generations, societies and their members mutually create one another, while providing the hope and courage needed by both as they confront the precarious passages of life.

Even enlightened church leaders have been slow to introduce the use of African names at baptism. In Zaire, the initiative came from the government of Mobutu Sese Seko when he decided to abandon his "Christian" names, Joseph Désiré, and retrieve from the dustbin of history his original African names. At the same time the Belgian Congo became Zaire. Leopoldville was renamed Kinshasa, and Elizabethville became Lulumbashi. To his lasting credit, the late Cardinal Malula of Kinshasa, after first resisting Mobutu's prohibition of foreign baptismal names, later became a leading advocate of Christianity's cultural indigenization in Africa.

Do the church's ministers everywhere accept the good news that African cultures are as acceptable to God as Jewish, European and North American cultures? If so, it is obviously appropriate to incorporate into the life of the church specifically African symbol systems. Thus it is fitting to encourage the use of traditional African names in the Christian rites of initiation. Names designating real human beings, not de-cultured abstractions called "souls," are common signs of cultural identity.

As Christian symbols, such traditional African names as Kamau, Saitoti, Lemalali, Nankunini and Ntina, will become cultural reminders of the good news that generations of deceased Africans bearing traditional names are also members of the corporately saved human family. They, no less than Christians, have been called by grace to the unity and salvation proclaimed by Jesus. If called by God, then they have not been denied the necessary means of responding to the call. For the means necessary for everyone, Christian or not, theist or not, we may consult the final judgment scene in the twenty-fifth chapter of the gospel according to Matthew. Considering the ubiquity of God's saving presence and Christianity's historical patterns of expansion in relation to the global distribution of humankind's population since the arrival of *homo sapiens* on the stage of history, we may assume that most of heaven's current inhabitants were identified on earth not by Jewish or European names, but by the indigenous names used in their respective bands, clans, tribes, peoples and nations.

A MONOPHYSITE TENDENCY

Although enlightened adaptations of the Roman rite have been made with respect to African cultural practices in many dioceses (e.g., African types of singing and dancing during liturgical ceremonies), it is astonishing how little liturgical use is made of traditional African prayer forms, practices, gestures, styles and imagery. By insisting generally upon prefabricated imports, usually learned and recited mechanically, the colonial methods of the church continue to devalue the religious heritage of Africans, while at the same time undermining the psychology of the prayer experience itself which is always rooted in a particular historico-cultural context.

Look, for example, at the sharp contrast between the typical Maasai prayers recorded in chapter three of this volume, and the bloodless abstractions found in the Roman Missal. A wooden conformity to archaic Roman ways appears normative in the Catholic liturgy where even the real bread of the eucharistic meal has been reduced to something resembling plastic wafers. Even classical European devotions and prayers can be misleading, sometimes degenerating into magic, superstition or crypto-heresy when presented in literalistic translations and without any understanding of their originating matrices.

Some presentations of Christianity place between God and humankind so many intermediaries—man-made historical accretions—that any word of revelation is apt to be obscured or distorted, if not lost in a maze of dated and culture-specific interpretations, ideologies, structures, institutions and practices. In some times and places, for example, so much emphasis is placed on the mother of Jesus, statues and the rosary, that she is apt to appear more important than Jesus, more powerful than the Holy Spirit, and perhaps even as a goddess, to people encountering Christianity for the first time. What are they to think when, with no adequate explanation, they are told to sing the praises of the mother of God? It seems a logical inference, especially among peoples accustomed to using feminine images for the divinity, that the mother of Jesus must be a goddess.

Exaggerated Marian devotions may be seen as a consequence of European Christianity's monophysite tendency to regard Jesus Christ simply as God, and thus to feel the need for a more human mediation than Jesus between God and humankind. So, a distinctly monophysite flavor in some forms of Christian piety has been noted by a number of contemporary theologians. Joseph Ratzinger, for example, has this to say about it:

> The truth of the humanity of Christ got left more and more in the shade in the course of the centuries, and in practice Jesus was seen only as God. So there occurred something like a conceal-ment (of his humanity), or a clear Monophysitism in Christian piety.[11]

Our hermeneutical principles, so necessary for our understanding of the Bible and the official teachings of the church, are relevant also in this realm of religious practices and pious customs. In this regard, Marian devotions, embellished with historically and culturally conditioned forms of metaphor and hyperbole, taken directly from a past period of European chivalry, deserves particular attention. It can happen, when sentimentality replaces theological reflection, that the essential difference is obscured between the reverence due to God and that given to one of his redeemed creatures. "Devotion to Mary," writes Michael Schmaus, "is not a sort of intermediate entity between devotion to God and reverence for the saints....It is in the line of the reverence due to the creature and is essentially different from the reverence due to God." If popular devotions transgress these grounds, they are "in formal contradiction to the doctrine of the Church."[12]

What, for example is apt to be taken as the theological meaning of the well-known medieval hymn in honor of "Our Lady Mary," *Salve Regina,* "Hail Holy Queen," when this prayer is used cross-culturally without any understanding of its original historical context and literary genre? Again, the comments of Michael Schmaus are instructive: "In a number of prayers in official use, such as the 'Hail Holy Queen,' titles are applied to Mary which in their original sense were predicated of Christ ('our life, our hope'); the normal rules of hermeneutics are to be observed in interpreting them."[13] The historico-cultural context of this particular hymn is the age of European chivalry in a theological climate of neo-monophysitism; the literary genre is culture-specific poetry. These factors make a great difference in the meanings communicated through such historically conditioned prayers.

The point about foreign symbols sometimes communicating unintended meanings may be illustrated by the existence in Kenya and Tanzania of a new religion called the *Dini ya Legio* (Religion of the Legion); officially it is called the Maria Legio Church.[14] This flourishing breakaway movement from the Catholic Church had its genesis in the Legion of Mary, imported from Ireland with the best of intentions and many good results. But it raises large questions about missionary methods and expectations. Was this Irish institution simply superimposed—as just one more alien patch on the imported clothing of African Christians—on the assumption that what works well in Ireland should work well everywhere?

This, if anything, is an example of what Bernard Lonergan calls "missionaries preaching their own culture." Is it appropriate to introduce such institutional systems, constructed to meet specifically European historical and cultural needs? Do Africans, in their many and varied cultural contexts, perhaps have very different needs and their own ways of meeting them; ways capable of being integrated into the service of the Christian community? Do imported solutions preempt the possibility of developing locally invented ways of promoting and supporting the Christian ministry? Whatever answers may come to mind, it is worth recalling that, instead of trying to solve historically and culturally conditioned human problems by importing divinely fashioned institutions, God's original missionary to humankind sought solutions, doubtless less efficient ones, in the existing cultural institutions of the particular people among whom he lived.

Emotional preaching, pious practices and devotions that leave the humanity, ethnicity, historicity, cultural conditioning, finitude and vulnerability of Jesus in the background, while dramatically emphasizing the exalted, powerful and triumphal presence of "almighty and eternal God" in him, undercut the significance of his entire human experience, and the intended meanings behind the historical mission of the divine Word. In consequence, as Yves Congar tried to tell us half a century ago, Jesus is apt to seem remote from our human lives, and we may feel a need for some sort of "really human" mediator between him and ourselves. And who could provide better mediation than his own mother? Now we all know, however, that the proposed dogmatic definition of Mary as the mediatrix of all graces, with its strong monophysite flavor and firm support from Catholic fundamentalists like the late Archbishop Marcel Lefebvre, was rejected by the fathers of Vatican Council II.

At the same time, Father Congar also warned us—and perhaps this is one reason why a long silence was imposed upon him in the years before the council—that a monophysite contaminated ecclesiology, pretending to be free of human finitude, historical constraints and cultural obtuseness, follows logically from a monophysite christology. Preaching, piety and devotions may lead people astray when, in Congar's words,

> The true humanity of Christ, together with that of the Church, is insufficiently emphasized....Where the Church in particular is

concerned, it is often forgotten that the hierarchical action, by which authority is exercised, while under the special guidance of the Spirit...is concretely the work of men carried out in circumstances of time, place and human resources, where normally the ordinary conditioning of the historical environment has full play.[15]

The interpretation by non-western peoples of exotic devotions, developed from European experiences and historical events, is especially problematical when two such devotions are combined and dramatized with processions, candles and incense; for example, the recitation of the rosary during benediction of the blessed sacrament. Leave aside for now the historical significance of the rosary which was introduced into thirteenth century Spain by the followers of Islam who had borrowed it from Buddhists. Adoration of the eucharist in the form of exposition and benediction, and the prolonged elevation of the sacramental species during mass, also emerged during the same medieval period in Europe. These practices were initially intended as an instructional reaction against a particular heresy of that historical time and place. In practice, however, this reaction to the eleventh-century theology of Berengarius of Tours may have done more than the teachings of Berengarius himself to distort the meaning of the eucharist, as a sacramental memorial of Christ's life, death, resurrection and unity with his followers. As Lucien Deiss reminds us, "it is so much easier to adore the real presence of Christ in the tabernacle than to venerate that same real presence in our neighbour's heart and surround it with love."[16]

The original significance of communion through a commemorative meal, requested by Jesus and modeled on the ritual meal of the Jewish Passover, was gradually superseded by the practice of adoring and petitioning God during the divinity's literal, physical, material, tangible and visible presence in the symbolic materials used in the rites of benediction and mass. This insistent literalism, with its stress on physical objectivity, and its emphatic focus on the elements used in the memorial meal, progressively obscured the original meaning of the eucharistic meal itself. Even Jesus tended to be seen simply as God present more under the appearance of these ritual elements than in the believing community, in the proclamation of the word, and in the suffering neighbor. The ostensorium and the tabernacle were treated like reliquaries containing relics of God who could be tangibly encountered especially during expositions of the "sacred species," just as the relics of saints were displayed as objects (physical things) for public veneration and for obtaining miracles. What was forgotten then, and still needs more emphasis today, is that "it is the eating, not the presence of the species, which is the sacramental sign."[17]

Against the persistent monophysite tendency reflected in the religious practices of western Christians, both Catholic and Reformed, it must be appreciated and adequately emphasized that Jesus Christ is not less but more truly human than all the rest of us. During his brief historical pilgrimage, he showed himself to be, unlike the rest of us sinners, just what God calls all of us to be: perfect as our heavenly Father is perfect, made and re-created by grace in the divine image. "In Christ," says Avery Dulles, "the manifestation and that which is manifested ontologically coincide. The man Jesus Christ is both the symbol and the incarnation of the eternal Logos, who communicates himself by becoming fully human without ceasing to be divine." In this way, Professor Dulles expresses the "classical" doctrine of the "two natures," as an "interlocked reality," in Christ:

> Christ's humanity is really identical with himself; it is not a mere mask for his divinity. But it is more than his humanity, and this more, according to Christian belief, is his divinity.[18]

A balanced christology, giving all due attention to the human nature of Christ and thus also to the human elements in the Church, will help us to be more like Christ, walking more humbly and less infallibly in the presence of God, and before the peoples with whom we are supposed to be sharing the good news of God's incarnate Word.

QUASI-PELAGIAN SPIRITUALITY

Another example of the distortions of Christianity introduced into parts of sub-Saharan Africa by missionaries is a form of spirituality, rooted in ancient Mediterranean Stoicism, and still bearing the marks of its chief pro-pagandist, Pelagius, a fifth-century British monk based in Rome.[19] Congenial to the western penchant for cost-effective measuring and calculating, this spirituality tends to underestimate the magnanimity of God; so it is nervously self-reliant in its orientation and practices. By multiplying religious acts and punctiliously observing all the rules devised by theologians, canon lawyers and liturgists for pleasing God, it is assumed that "more grace" can be obtained, and the chances of final salvation will be more assured. This accu-mulation of quantified "grace" builds self-assurance and feelings of right-eousness when such good and pious people regard their own strengths, devo-tion and faithfulness over against the laxity or sluggishness of ordinary Christians. Hard-working piety of this sort is joyless; it may even yield sadness at the Lord's magnanimity shown to those arriving in the vineyard only at the eleventh hour (cf. Matthew 20:1–16).

Such a spirituality is apt to influence negatively the Christian understanding of the sacraments. When people use a conceptual model through which the sacraments are seen as isolated and vertical encounters between the individual and God, the sacramental action appears as a "good work," and its repetition is supposed to "increase grace" as saving power in and for the individual. It is erroneously assumed that God's saving love is brought about or somehow made more available in these ritual enactments than elsewhere; also that the efficacy of the action, and an increase in the "amount" of grace, is achieved *ipso facto* by the frequency of the sacramental enactments. It is "almost a magical idea that the more often we receive the sacraments the better, provided only that a right intention and a certain amount of good will are present, to increase the 'treasury of grace' through the sacraments." Rahner's point here deserves more attention than it usually gets:

> Any merely numerical accumulation of such receptions of the sacraments becomes meaningless. In no conceivable sense does it really increase grace, and it leads merely to a legalistic and mechanistic approach to the sacramental event.[20]

This may be basically a question of where the emphasis should be placed in our understanding of God's saving grace. The focus upon the disposition and expectation of the individual recipient of the sacraments may obscure the primary significance of the ritual enactment, namely, that "what is brought to effective manifestation in the dimension of the Church in the sacraments is precisely *that* grace which, in virtue of God's universal will to save, is effective everywhere in the world where humankind does not react to it with absolute denial."[21] The Christian believer, as Christ's witness, stands here symbolically (sacramentally) for all who respond to God's offer, while the church's ritual enactment signifies the offer of grace to all of humankind. The recipient of the sacrament is here engaged in a representative role. So, Father Rahner can assure us that every offer and response to grace is always on behalf of others:

> Those who explicitly belong to the visible Church are not so much those who are called and predestined to salvation....Rather, they are those who, through their life, their confessing, their membership of the Church, have to make salvation manifest sacramentally to those *others* within the solidarity which embraces all people

within a human race which has been redeemed by Christ. The members of the Church in a true sense work out their salvation precisely *in that* they fulfill to the full this function which they have regarding the rest.[22]

PRIVATIZING SPIRITUALITY

An appreciation of the dignity of each individual, and an increasing concern with the sanctity of each one's human and civil rights, is a hard-won and historically recent achievement of Euro-American culture. Through the relevant insights and articulations of this late western culture, it is possible and desirable to share this value with peoples whose cultures and social structures, in response to various historical pressures and the harsh demands of precarious subsistence economies, have tended to give far more attention to a people's corporate destiny and collective survival. This, as illustrated by current events in several countries of the south, sometimes results in the blatant neglect or abuse of the basic human and civil rights of individuals, especially those who happen to belong to the "wrong" ethnic groups, social classes, political parties or religions.

Still, it must be recognized that an excessive emphasis upon the individual, an emphasis characterizing the attitudes and practices of late western Christianity in both its Catholic and Protestant manifestations, sometimes called "nineteenth century individualism"[23] tends to be a disintegrating force in African cultural worlds. An excessive emphasis on the individual contradicts the essential social nature of humanity. It is, in any case, a distortion of Christianity's own primordial sense of humankind's corporate solidarity and common destiny.

This individualism, brought to Africa by missionaries, propagated by a narrow concept of sin with little social consciousness, and reinforced by the western acquisitiveness inculcated through schooling, is described by contemporary Catholic theologians as "a major distortion of the Christian religion." This individualistic interpretation of Christianity's good news amounts to a privatization of religion; it tends to legitimate the atomization of the traditional social order, undermining cooperative practices, promoting competitiveness, and fostering an attitude of "each individual for himself."[24] These may be virtues derived from the western world's modern economic system, but they are hardly the virtues urged by Jesus.

Indeed, this Euro-American culture of selfish individualism, is less congenial to Christian living than many traditional African cultures. It is, as a threatening world-culture, "totalitarian," "technocratic," "materialistic," and "secularizing." According to this analysis by anthropologist and long-time missionary in Africa, Aylward Shorter, it is at the macro-level a "universal anti-culture," devoid of human substance, and lacking its own lived tradition. Moreover, it "continues to widen the gap between rich and poor," to promote urbanization, to undermine religious and moral values, to wipe out traditions, and to jeopardize the post-colonial resurgence of the south.[25]

The New Testament does not present Jesus as the personal and private savior of each individual in separation from all the others, as though each were standing alone and naked before the almighty and eternal God; much less does it correlate wealth and power with divine favor. No. Before a forgiving God, humanity has a compassionate advocate. Jesus is the normative symbol of God's saving love for all peoples, the whole of humankind, from the beginning of human history to the end inclusively. Even the Christ-event in history is itself an efficacious consequence of that divine magnanimity.

So the efficacy of God's saving love for his creatures is neither determined nor limited by the historical accident of each individual's time and place of birth, nor by the early or late arrival, here or there, of missionaries from Europe or North America. It is not primarily a matter of each one's psychologically personal and explicit encounter with Jesus. The kingdom preached by Jesus is an eschatological collectivity embracing all of humankind, and God's saving love inundates all, whether people know about this or not. In principle, therefore, all are saved already in virtue of the universal and loving presence of God's Spirit, although each one is free to reject the offer of salvation and unity of which Jesus is the tangible pledge in these "latter days." Rejection is always a function of selfish individualism. This is the exact opposite of being in accord with the example of Jesus, the "man for others" (Bonhoeffer).

The message of Jesus is not about saving "souls" for an afterlife in some ethereal paradise. Nor is Jesus to be seen as a medicine man sent to solve miraculously the local problems of each individual who would invoke his assistance. "He came," says Gregory Baum, "to usher in a new age that would transform the very structure of human life."[26] Transformation, we must recall, does not mean destruction and substitution. It is more like the activity of a tiny measure of yeast working gradually within a mass of dough. This is an appropriate New Testament image of Christ; it is an action model for those sent by him. They are supposed to function as the leaven of the gospel transforming cultures from within.

Such is the Christian self-understanding reflected in the documents of Vatican II. The world is seen as the theater of humanity's history, bearing the marks of human energies, achievements, tragedies, failures and triumphs. In the Christian view, this world of ours is created and sustained by divine love. Although fallen into the bondage of sin, it is also emancipated by Christ, "so that it might be fashioned anew and reach its fulfillment in accord with God's design." Because the community of Christian believers "travels the same journey as the rest of humankind and shares the same earthly lot with everyone else, the Church is supposed to be a leaven, as it were, the soul of human society in its renewal...."[27]

Christianity, far from being an other-worldly preoccupation with rescuing "souls" from all the wickedness of our planetary village, is concerned primarily with the human affairs of this very planet. Not only did God make the world of humankind, but he so loves this world that he is always and everywhere re-creating it by the loving action of the Holy Spirit. This good news of God's self-bestowal in and for the whole of creation, has even been dramatized for us in concrete human history by the sending of the divine Word and Spirit in Jesus Christ who, however fully glorified now in the life of the divinity, is still a human being, and our ever-present mediator with God. Instead of running from the world, Christians, in response to the impulses of the Spirit and in obedience to the mission of Christ, are supposed to function as a transforming leaven and a universally intelligible sign of the coming reign of God.

Belief in the incarnation of the divine Word, with all of its disconcerting implications, is the key to understanding the Christian way of transformation; it is also a light cast upon the transcendent meaning of mundane existence. Thus we learn that God is not found by looking beyond the historico-cultural order of finite existence and bypassing the actual human condition as it is. Rather, God is mediated to us only through humanity in its worldly context, because the absoluteness and transcendence of God has been inserted into this ephemeral context. In the words of Karl Rahner, "what takes place in Jesus Christ with a preeminent fullness applies essentially, though in a minor and modified degree, to the world in general which God takes into his grace." Thus, "a right and full relationship with the world (which is, above all, a world of personal communicating in love and freedom) is in itself a relationship...with God himself." Once more, the reason for the present supernatural (grace-filled, saved, redeemed in principle) order of human existence is that, by the way of incarnation, God has lovingly and freely inserted himself into this world of his own making.[28]

The most earthshaking consequence of this divine-human unity—and this is Christianity's signal challenge to all culturally structured religious systems, with their multiple human rules and practices, including those of Christianity itself—is the new consciousness produced by the explicit revelation of the unity of the love of neighbor and the love of God. People intensely engaged in the practices of their inherited religions, saving themselves by consciously multiplying these pious actions (e.g., some of the Jews in the time of Jesus, and some Christians ever since then) sometimes have more trouble seeing this truth than others who are either downright impious or sluggish in their religious rule-keeping. This is why the scandalous impression is sometimes given by pious and devout souls in the quasi-Pelagian tradition that the more religious one's behavior, the more distant one is apt to be from the kernel of Christ's message.

The plight of such people is tragic, because the New Testament is abundantly clear about this, that the only explicit standard by which persons will be saved or damned, is the love shown to one's neighbor in need (Matthew 25:34–46). Since the neighbor in need is identified with Jesus Christ, the God-Man himself, the divinity-in-humanity, there is no other way of salvation, and no substitute for this particular act of love. This is a recurring theme of Rahner's, optimistic understanding of grace, and it is central to his whole theological enterprise, against which some theologians still imagine that "grace would no longer be grace if God became too free with it."[29]

The foregoing notes on the symbolism of names, the monophysite tendency, quasi-Pelagianism and excessive individualism suggest some of the reasons for the church's questionable image in Africa today. The image remains overwhelmingly alien with a highly individualistic focus on exotic laws, rules, concepts, practices, unexamined assumptions and unintelligible formulations of belief. The anomaly is dramatized in some mission stations and parishes by imported statues of lifelike painted plaster. Devoid of artistic merit even by western standards, these curiosities are more reminiscent of Mediterranean polytheism than of the New Testament. Widely presented in the dazzling garb of foreign wealth and power, Christianity appears as a superior tribal religion striving to displace, and substitute for, the traditional religions of the peoples. Up to now, there is almost no dialogue with the indigenous religious heritage, much less collaboration or inculturation. It is as though the most solemn mandates of the Second Vatican Council nearly three decades ago have been sabotaged by some of the very people responsible for their implementation.

MORE PLURALISM NEEDED

Instead of importing more foreign-bred ideologies and alien accoutrements of religion, thereby partly burying the real meaning of Christianity's good news and sometimes reducing it to bad news, Lonergan's culturally sensitive missionary, acknowledging a multiplicity of valid and graced cultures, would "proceed from within" the local culture. Together with the people themselves, he or she would seek ways and means of transforming indigenous systems into vehicles for illuminating, communicating and supporting the meaning of God's good news.[30]

Not only the indigenous prayer forms but the whole culture of a people should be seen as valid and indispensable for the realization of the church's incarnational mission. A culture is a complex of symbol systems, embodying, codifying and communicating a humanly constructed and historically transmitted pattern of meanings, values, perceptions, ideas, attitudes, myths, judgments, aspirations, beliefs, commitments and actions through which the experience of reality is mediated, interpreted coherently and structured consistently. No human being exists—whether Cro-Magnon man, Baptist preacher or Hindu guru—outside of some such inherited symbol system which not only mediates the person's experience of reality, but also provides the identity and prescribes the conduct of each one. The person is reached only in and through his or her ephemeral cultural world: not by substituting for it the cultural world of some other people, ancient or modern. Of all the components of culture, "religion," as George Bernard Shaw reminds us, "is a great force—the only real motive force in the world." Missionaries and pastors especially should take note of Shaw's next line: "What you fellows don't understand is that you must get at a man through his religion and not through yours."[31]

If God truly enlightens every one that comes into this world (cf. John 1:9, 16), proffering divine friendship to each member of the human family (cf.1 Timothy 2:4); if people are expected to respond to this grace in a free and human manner, thus allowing for the possibility of rejection through an evil decision of conscience, then this must happen in the concretely available terms and conditions of each person's historical moment and cultural context. This is why cultures, including their religious components, must be taken seriously for what they are in themselves; why, indeed, the missionary enterprise must focus not on isolated individuals abstracted from their actual situations of time and place, but on persons within their own cultural worlds and historical periods. The cultures themselves are supposed to be evangelized and assumed by the church. This is not done by some superficial manipulation, nor by token gestures of acceptance, much less by substituting one cultural invention for another. Rather, it is to be done in the same radically accepting way that is signified by the incarnation of God's Word in Jesus of Nazareth.

No authentic cultural system is foreign to the Holy Spirit, although some cultures, during particular periods of their histories, may indeed be more resistant than others to the gospel of Jesus. Nor is there any reason to believe that the Spirit speaks and acts more efficaciously in Judaic, Hellenic, Coptic, Roman, Iberian, Teutonic, Slavic, Gallic, Celtic or Anglo-Saxon terms than in the terms of any ethnic-culture group in Africa, Asia or the Islands far away. The cultural patterns of the peoples being evangelized are all under the same universal Lord of history, hence inundated by the same re-creating and superabounding grace of God. All cultures are presumed to be compatible with Christianity, even though all are defective and always in need of healing grace. This compatibility need not be proven beforehand. The burden of proof rests with anyone who suspects that a particular cultural element may be totally incompatible with Christian faith. The presumption is always in favor of the indigenous ways of being human and religious.

11

A Radically New Attitude

From now on the Church opens her door and becomes the house which all may enter, and in which all can feel at home, while keeping their own culture and traditions, provided these are not contrary to the Gospel. —Pope John Paul II [1]

During almost the entire history of Christianity, up to the second half of the twentieth century, ecclesiastical officialdom has generally frowned upon the countless other religions that have always served the vast majority of people on our planet. Even academic theologians, with relatively few exceptions, have tended to ignore the history of religions other than their own particular versions of Christianity. Now, however, it appears with increasing clarity that the other religions, once considered merely natural at best, satanic at worst, will continue to serve an ever-increasing majority of humankind. Now also, thanks in great measure to the explicit proclamation of the theological implications of the Second Vatican Council's hopeful teaching on the condition of non-Christians and their religions, vis-à-vis God's saving love for humankind, the official attitude of the Catholic Church has been altered radically. In varying degrees this wider ecumenism is reflected in the writings of contemporary theologians and in the more open attitudes of increasing numbers of Christians.

The call of the church today is, in the words of Pope John Paul II, for

28

"'dialogue' with the cultures and religious values of the different peoples" constituting the human family. Far from ignoring these values, much less scorning them, we are obliged to seek in them "the 'seeds of the Word,' to be found in human initiatives—including religious ones—and in people's efforts to attain truth, goodness and God himself."[2] Things like this have been said before in the course of the Church's long history, but never so frequently and hardly with the same insistence seen since the end of the Second Vatican Council in 1965. Nor is this just a Catholic thing.

The new-found ecumenical attitudes of Catholics and Protestants during the post-Vatican II period gradually led to a more confident recognition of Jews "as comembers of God's covenants." With an unavoidable logic, we are now facing what Langdon Gilkey calls "some sort of parity" with all the other religions in a much wider ecumenism. This new attitude requires "the elimination of our assumption of unquestioned or a priori superiority of our religion," and it entails "the recognition that each has something to hear and to learn from the others in dialogue." So it is that both Catholics and Protestants today are trying "to think out a new Christian theology of the encounter of faiths."[3]

This bold acceptance of humanity's invincible cultural pluralism proclaims Christianity's need to express its faith in the diverse terms of each people's own historico-cultural world. Although still only theoretical, this position is more fully incarnational than what is signified by the translation and/or substitution model reflected in the work of most missionaries and pastors in Africa.[4] In the face of cultural diversity, Walter Brueggemann considers a Protestant perspective to be more inclined to a "hermeneutic of suspicion," while a Catholic perspective is more inclined to a "constructive appreciation of cultural embodiment."[5] This is surely the key issue addressed by the principle of inculturation: whether or to what extent Christian faith is supposed to bypass, negate or affirm the claims any culture has on the loyalty of its people.

One reason for the differing inclinations of Catholic and Protestant approaches to cultural pluralism is, of course, the definitive significance attributed to the words of the Bible in the Protestant tradition, hence the urgency of translating these words into the various vernaculars of the world. Aside from this primary concern with the linguistic component of every culture, the "Christ-against-culture" stance (in H.R. Niebuhr's typology) appears more congenial to Protestants than to Catholics. Another reason, suggested by Yves Congar, is the greater degree of attention Catholics are apt to give to the mystery of the incarnation, specifically to its this-worldly, historico-cultural and liturgical implications.[6] A third reason is the sea change experienced by modern Catholics in their renewed understanding of saving grace as God's self-communication (self-revelation) always and everywhere among all peoples.

Thanks to theologians like Karl Rahner, whose understanding of grace is reflected not only in the documents of Vatican II but also in the 1990 encyclical letter *Redemptoris missio,* we see now more clearly than in the past that "the Holy Spirit offers everyone the possibility of sharing in the Paschal Mystery in a manner known to God...and that humanity is being continually stirred by the Spirit of God" who is at the very origin of humankind's existential and religious imagining, wondering, questioning, searching, building, believing, praying and celebrating—thus affecting "not only individuals but also society, history, peoples, cultures and religions." It is now recognized officially that "every authentic prayer is prompted by the Holy Spirit who is mysteriously present in every human heart." This same Spirit who gives life to the church also "implants and develops his gifts in all individuals and peoples." This Spirit is today "guiding the...church to discover these gifts, to foster them and to receive them through dialogue" with the followers of the other religions. The church's positive relationship with these religions is thus "dictated by...respect for humankind's quest for answers to the deepest questions of human life, and respect for the action of the Spirit in people."[7]

THE WAY OF INCARNATION AND DIALOGUE

As indicated by the foregoing words of Pope John Paul II, the ubiquity and magnanimity of the Holy Spirit—or the divine will that all of humankind, made originally in the image of God, should be re-created by divine love—is the inspiration for the new attitude toward all human cultures and their religious components. But the growing body of relevant literature gives at least equal emphasis to the role of the divine Word in the tangible realm of finitude, flesh, history and culture. From the birth, life, ministry, suffering, death and resurrection of Jesus of Nazareth—the primordial missionary of God's good news for humankind—is derived the missionary principle nowadays called "inculturation," although the documents of Vatican II used the classical theological term "incarnation" which is certainly more radical in its connotations and implications; it is also less easily reduced to pure conceptualism.

The key to a proper understanding of the Christian world mission is Jesus of Nazareth, particularly how his humanity and the events of his life are interpreted. Whether approaching this heroic figure from below, through the relevant historical and cultural data demonstrating his authentic humanity and time-conditioned Jewishness; or from above, through the Easter faith-claims of his associates, we are apt to arrive at the same place. In theological shorthand this place is traditionally called the mystery of the incarnation. "This is," in the words of Karl Rahner, "the very center of the reality from which we Christians live...."[8] So, this is our point of departure, as it was for the fathers of the Second Vatican Council in their treatment of the church's nature and missionary outreach.

Attentive to the "signs of the times," it was certainly a primary concern of the Second Vatican Council, facing the third world in a post-colonial era, to show a maximum respect for humanity's invincible historical diversity and cultural pluriformity. Hence the council's emphasis on the primordial and unique principle of incarnation, only recently designated by the neologism "inculturation."[9] The communication of the divine Word to humankind, as also any human response, presupposes mutual historical conditioning and cultural enfleshment of the communicants. People exist only in limited historical periods, and within concrete cultural contexts, all with their respective symbol systems of communication. God's dynamic self-communication, which we call grace, always has an incarnational tendency. There is an indispensable need for fleshly visibility, audibility and tangibility in particular historical and cultural forms capable of mediating the meaning of God's Word in the respective times and contexts of each distinctive people. This is why the church is now striving for a new openness to all peoples, and why the church aspires to become "the house...in which all may feel at home."[10] At least in theory, if not yet fully in practice, all peoples are free to be themselves in the church, each distinctive people with their own cultures and traditions; free in everything except sin.

In spite of much historical, cultural and sociological evidence to the contrary—including the monoculturalism of ecclesiastical law, persisting even in the 1983 revision of the code of canon law, not to mention various ethnocentric signals from some of the church's servants in both high and low places—the formal teachings of Vatican II assure us unambiguously that the church "is not tied exclusively or indissolubly to any race or nation, to any one particular way of life, ancient or modern"...but is instead engaged in "a wonderful exchange in keeping with the economy of the incarnation."[11]

It is precisely by entering "into communion with different forms of culture, thereby enriching both itself and the cultures themselves,"[12] that the church is enabled to grow in catholicity while serving obediently its mission to every tribe and tongue and people and nation. Far from being historically static and culturally monolithic, the church, aspiring to become an authentically catholic sign of humankind's unity and salvation, "must implant itself among these groups—the large and distinct groups united by enduring ties, ancient religious traditions, and strong social relationships—*in the same way that Christ by his incarnation committed himself to the particular social and cultural circumstances of the people among whom he lived.*"[13] We used to think of the church as "catholic" while it was in fact quite "provincial" in its cultural-specific garb, archaic language and idiosyncratic posturing. Although always intentionally catholic in an abstract sense, the church is now trying to come alive, indeed to be born into, the much larger cultural worlds outside of Europe and North America. At least it is more widely recognized today that "the real challenge of the Christian faith comes from within," as Raimundo Panikkar puts it, "from the inner dynamic toward universality, from its own claim to 'catholicity.'"[14]

This principle of incarnation, oriented toward catholicity, is derived directly from the scandalous belief that God in Jesus became one of us in *everything* except sin (cf. Hebrews 2:14–18; 4:15). This belief governs the Christian understanding of the relationship between God and humankind. God so loves the world that he (she/it) assumed human nature from the inside, embracing a mode of existence not his previously.[15] Through this incomprehensible and self-emptying humility (cf. Philippians 2:6–8), the divine Word became fully one of us in human finitude, flesh, history: like ourselves in our daily experience, circumscribed by the particularity of time, place, ethnicity and culture, while thinking, learning, acting and loving with a human mind, will and heart. Jesus of Nazareth is not a disguise used by God, not a human outer garment covering the divinity, not something foreign or extrinsic to what we are. This theme of incarnation dominates the religious experience and self-understanding of Christians uncontaminated by the quasi-monophysite pietisms inherited from late medieval Europe, and vigorously asserted in some modern forms of both Catholic and Protestant fundamentalism.

THE CHURCH AS MISSION

The action of God disclosed in the life of Jesus is paradigmatic for the church's ministry. What God has done through Jesus Christ once and for all in the historico-cultural terms of one particular people, the church must do among all peoples who, with their richly varied experiences and myriad cultural achievements, stand symbolically for, and indeed constitute—today, yesterday and tomorrow—the whole of humankind in its spatio-temporal extension. As Jesus Christ is the sacrament of God, so the church is the sacrament of Christ manifesting tangibly, in the fleeting terms of history and culture, the hidden but victorious and superabounding gift of God's Spirit (uncreated grace) at work always and everywhere. This Spirit is intimately present to all peoples in a manner analogous to a friendly breeze embracing us, or to the air we breathe.[16]

Indeed, this is why the church exists: to body forth herself in the sight of each people, so that all may see who they themselves really are, also who and what the church really is: God's own people reunited in a second Adam situation. This is a new solidarity of humankind re-created by the Spirit in accord with the Word of God. The Word is sent in Jesus to make known this good news in historical and cultural intelligibility among all peoples. In turn, the believing community is sent to one new people after another. Theirs is the task, as described by Karl Rahner, of making Christ present symbolically in his words and deeds "among all peoples as such in their own specific histories and cultures, and thereby achieving a quite new incarnational presence of Christ himself in the world."[17] Such is the mission; its completion is now entrusted to the whole community of Christian believers. A Christian, therefore, is one who is chosen for mission. In the words of Joseph Ratzinger: "Election is always at bottom election for others. For the Church, as for the individual, election is identical with the missionary obligation."[18]

This perception of God's ecumenical purpose in history contains both the motive and the method of the church's missionary outreach. It defines the church not as the kingdom of God on earth; not as people holier than others; not as an end in itself, but as a means. It is "an instrument" of the incarnational mission of the divine Word in Christ to all nations.[19] Instead of thinking of the church having a mission, we might think of the mission having a church. This community of believers is a means of serving the mission. Such a view of the church suggests more clearly the dynamic nature and purpose of the believing community, united with Christ in one body, symbolically representing all peoples, as a part standing for the whole, and reaching out to all.

According to the First Vatican Council, the church is "a sign raised up among the nations inviting all who have not yet believed." Believed what exactly? That, in spite of all that divides peoples (ethnically, culturally, historically, religiously, economically, politically, geographically) we really are one people of God, made in the divine image. Although it is not yet recognized universally, the common destiny of each people and of every individual consists somehow in this hopeful, if elusive, family unity to which all are

invited. We say "somehow," because the way of wooden conformity exter-
nally imposed, so widely employed by the church up to now, does not lead to
real unity, and the incarnational way of pluriformity, allowing people to be
themselves in everything except sin, has yet to be tried extensively.

So, in obedience to this mission of the divine Word, the church also
must go out of herself, emptying herself of power, foreign riches and alien
accretions, opening herself to pluriform modes of existence not hers previously; thus humbling herself in order to assume, experience, express and celebrate a new life (new creation) in the physical and cultural flesh of all the
other peoples among whom she does not yet exist indigenously. The church,
in other words, is supposed to make herself completely at home among each
people in the same authentically human way that Jesus was at home in
Nazareth, in everything except sin.

This does not mean that every single positive element of a particular
people's culture must find its formal place in the local community's expression of Christianity, but that everything should be accepted by the local
church in a manner analogous to the acceptance of the ancient Jewish cultural world by Jesus and his first followers. Nor does this mean that among each
particular people every individual in numerical computability must become a
Christian. This is not possible, because so many individuals have died, and
will die, before the advent of the church as an intelligible sign raised up
among them in the cultural terms of their own people. The church does not,
indeed cannot, function tangibly as a hopeful sign among the nations always
and everywhere simultaneously. But it does so exist, at least consecutively as
a "little flock," in the gradually unfolding terms of history among one people
after another. So it has been since the significant events of the first Pentecost.

The church's presence to a people must have the character of dialogue,
according to the model of the divine Word who "pitched his tent among us"
(John 1:14) and behaved, without pretensions, in his own authentically
human manner conditioned by ethnicity, history and culture. This ecclesial
presence is not built upon the people's uncritical acceptance of all the formulas, rules, rituals, books and practices carried from abroad in the baggage of
missionaries. First and last, this presence must be in the form of human
encounter which achieves understanding only to the extent that people are
accepted for what they are in their own circumscribed histories and limited
cultures; and to the extent the church's functionaries are authentically themselves in human terms, without pretending to be what they are not.

"Encounter," says Bernard Lonergan, "is meeting persons, appreciating the values they represent, criticizing their defects, and allowing one's living to be challenged at its very roots by their words and by their deeds."[20]

This humble attitude of openness and honesty is quite the opposite of paranoid apologetics, defending the institutional church by trying to cover up or explain away our ecclesial history of typical human weakness, folly, arrogance, careerism, political maneuvering, brutality, simony and idiosyncratic posturing. The church of "saints and sinners at the same time" is not yet the completed church, "without spot or wrinkle," of God's eschatological kingdom. Unavoidably, the weeds and the wheat continue to grow together until the end. Surely, the people of the church still have much to learn from the others among whom the Spirit is also at work always and everywhere.

HISTORICAL PERSPECTIVES

The missionary principle of incarnation, although variously formulated and frequently ignored throughout the ages of the church's history, may be traced back to its earliest application in St. Paul's missionary ministry modeled on the mission of the divine Word spoken to humankind in Jesus of Nazareth. The apostle to the gentiles was challenged, and indeed hounded until his death, by a party of Jewish Christians who had erroneously confused Christianity with their own ethnic conventions and cultural practices, which they wished to impose upon all non-Jewish converts to Christianity (cf. Acts 15:1–30; 17:22–28; Galatians 2:1–4). Vindicated by Paul, the principle was applied generously in the Greco-Roman cultural world. The consequent fusion of Christianity with Mediterranean cultures is a classic example, unsurpassed since then, of religious syncretism, at least on the surface.[21] In the course of time, and at a deeper level, this has been interpreted as an epochal instance of inculturation.

"To retain its life," says Frances Young, "religion needs to be earthed in a culture." This is so, because any religion is kept alive through the symbols, myths, images, and ritual celebrations of its followers in their respective historico-cultural terms. According to Professor Young, "it was because Christianity shared so much with paganism and could take on the values of traditional religion that it was able to replace its rivals." Early Christianity "assimilated the old festivals, images and symbols to its own view of appropriate worship, and was able to use paganism's own fundamental perceptions to justify and effect this."[22]

The early church's incarnationalism in the Mediterranean basin may be illustrated by its assumption and transformation of the pre-Christian celebration of the birth of the unconquerable sun (*natalis solis invicti*). It is a widely held theory that, by deliberately choosing to celebrate the birth of the Son at

the time of the traditional sun feast during the winter solstice—thus analogically applying to Jesus all the life-giving implications of the sun's arrival:
invincible light, warmth, comfort, renewal, hope—a popular pre-Christian
feast was appropriated and transformed into the most popular of Christian
celebrations. Scholars have also noted pre-Christian connections with the
Christian feast of the Epiphany: "it has affinities in place and time with the
Egyptian celebrations of the birth of Aion, the god of time and eternity."[23]
The so-called Hellenization of Christian doctrine is another example of the
incarnational way of Christianity making itself at home in one particular historico-cultural world. Hellenic conceptual systems were the available vehicles for intelligible communication in that particular context. It is a mistake,
however, to imagine that these philosophical systems are adequate to the
needs of all peoples of every time and place. Hellenism, as Bernard
Lonergan reminds us, "has very real limitations." These limitations "have
been transcended by modern culture," but they "have yet to be successfully
surmounted by Catholic theology."[24] Something similar might be said of
church law, much of which was taken bodily from pre-Christian Roman law.

The Pauline respect and creative boldness in the face of multiple cultural differences was not altogether abandoned when Christianity, together
with its Jewish and Greco-Roman accretions came to life among the other
peoples of Europe beyond the Mediterranean basin. If not a complete
inculturation of Christianity in these regions, there was at least a notable
measure of tolerance and patience. Various Teutonic, Iberian, Gallic,
Scandinavian, Celtic, Anglo-Saxon, and Slavic forms were allowed to find
their way into a more or less homogeneous Christendom. After its original
Judaic enfleshment, this Europeanization was the Christian community's
second epochal embodiment in the ephemeral cultural forms and historically conditioned structures, systems and institutions of the north.

When it came to missionary activity beyond the borders of ancient
Christendom, however, European ethnocentrism was particularly recalci-
trant. Church leaders were blinded by what Bernard Lonergan calls the
"classicist mentality."[25] Western culture, owing much to its ancient Greco-
Roman antecedents, was uncritically assumed to be normative for the
entire human family. Christians from other cultural worlds were expected,
indeed required, sometimes in the name of "divine law," to abandon their
own traditional ways of being human and religious. They were then morally coerced into embracing the "superior" ways of Europe, uncritically
imagined to be somehow more compatible with Christianity than the ways
invented and developed by most of humanity living outside of Europe.

For example, the Catholics of Goa in India, evangelized by St. Francis

Xavier and his associates in the sixteenth century, were victims of this European cultural arrogance masquerading as God's will. The Goans, responding to the "good news" brought by these Jesuit missionaries, were thus deprived not only of their immemorial traditions, but even of their indigenous names. The Christians were required to take not only the names of foreign saints, but also Portuguese or Spanish surnames such as DeSouza and Fernandes. This, together with many other foreign cultural impositions, including even hair styles, amounted to a massive psychosocial assault against the people's original cultural identity, self-understanding, ethos, worldview, aesthetic sense and human dignity.

The history of the expansion of Christianity is replete with such examples, confirming the truth of the observation made by the distinguished historian of religion, Wilfred Cantwell Smith: "The fundamental flaw of Western civilization in its role in world history is arrogance...and this has infected also the Christian church."[26] Perhaps the crudest recorded instance of this arrogance is the 1452 papal bull, *Dum diversis,* of Pope Nicholas V. In this document, His Holiness generously gave to the King of Portugal "full and entire faculty of invading, conquering, expelling and reigning over all the kingdoms...of the Saracens, of pagans, and of infidels, wherever they may be found; of reducing their inhabitants to perpetual slavery; of appropriating to yourself those kingdoms and all their possessions for your own use and that of your successors."[27] Papal rhetoric, as noted earlier in this chapter, is quite the opposite these days. But the destruction sanctioned by Nicholas has continued into the present century, albeit with methods progressively less brutal than those employed by the *conquistadores* of previous centuries.

Later missionaries, following the lead of Matteo Ricci (d. 1610) in China, and Roberto de Nobili (d.1656) in India, were more sensitive, morally, theologically and culturally, in their efforts to present Christianity's really good news in the cultural terms of their hearers, and with all due respect. Their enlightened approach yielded promising results, even spectacular results in the case of China.[28] But the Pauline boldness of these innovating Jesuits was upsetting to the "classicist mentality" of many missionary colleagues from other religious orders. So these incarnational approaches were plagued by controversies, calumnies and accusations similar to those suffered by St. Paul in his struggle with the ethnocentrism of the Judaizing Christians in his time.

The debate over the Jesuit efforts to make Christianity completely at home in China and in India, while making Chinese and Indian Christians at home in the church, was finally terminated in the middle of the eighteenth century by order of Pope Benedict XIV. This time, in contrast to the earlier decision at the so-called council of Jerusalem favoring St. Paul's missionary method, the decision was against the cultural catholicization of the church. Since then, western monoculturalism—basically, the historical experiences, myths, symbols, customs, assumptions, conceptions, arts, practices, laws and institutions of Europeans—has been regarded as normative for Christians everywhere in the world.

Where the Judaizers had failed the Europeanizers triumphed. Since then, notes Karl Rahner,

> the actual concrete activity of the Church in its relation to the world outside of Europe was in fact (if you will pardon the expression) the activity of an export firm which exported a European religion as a commodity it did not really want to change but sent throughout the world together with the rest of this supposedly superior culture and civilization....[29]

Although lip service was often given to the principle of incarnation, this is usually taken to mean literal translations and cautious adaptations. As in the past, a few indigenous cultural tokens are considered tolerable in practice. But missionary work continues to be reduced to establishing and maintaining western spiritual colonies throughout the non-western world. The cultural imperialism of Protestants has been no less tenacious than that of Catholics. So Robert Schreiter's challenging question is a recurring one wherever Christianity's missionary outreach is discussed today among both its advocates and its opponents: "Do we really mean what we say, or is it a subterfuge for carrying on a translation model of evangelization under a different name?"[30]

TOWARD AN AFRICAN CHRISTIANITY

The Second Vatican Council, by retrieving and reaffirming the incarnational principle, promised to put the Church back on its original course of authentic involvement with the whole inhabited earth. Christianity since then, in spite of significant resistance noted in both high and low places, has sometimes appeared to be on the verge of a third epochal enfleshment as a world church honestly embodied in the varied cultural symbol systems of humankind's vast majority existing in the non-western world.

The Vatican Secretariat for non-Christian religions, now called the

Pontifical Council for Interreligious Dialogue, has elaborated on the practical implications of this new appreciation of all religions. This Secretariat has twice addressed in detail the questions arising from the church's worldwide evangelizing mission in relation to the urgent need to initiate dialogue with the followers of these religions. Just three years after the close of the Second Vatican Council, the Secretariat for Non-Christians, under the presidency of Cardinal Paul Marella, published a book setting forth the Secretariat's position regarding African traditional religions. This document, *Meeting the African Religions,* presents an anthropological understanding of African religions, and it represents a significant theological step beyond the more generalized position of Vatican II: "If God is at work in the traditional African religions, and if man responds to this divine activity, the African religions contain an element of revelation, and the help of divine grace...."[31]

In 1988, the Nigerian Cardinal Francis Arinze, president of the Secretariat for Non-Christians, reminded the bishops of Africa and Madagascar of the church's proclaimed esteem for "the religions and cultures of various peoples," and the church's keen desire "in her contact with those peoples, to preserve all that is noble, true and good in their religions and cultures." Recalling the mandate of the Second Vatican Council, the Cardinal specified the particular aspects of these religions to be studied systematically in each cultural area by scholars chosen for their competence. Among the reasons given for the urgency of this research, Cardinal Arinze noted that "the underlying felt needs of Africans will be identified, so that it will become clear how Christianity can meet such needs, thus enabling the people to become more at home in the Church." This research is to be undertaken with a view to "deeper evangelization and deeper theological reflection," thereby identifying "elements which Christianity could adopt, or adapt, or ennoble and purify, or elements which it must reject."[32]

A full decade earlier, Cardinal Maurice Otunga of Kenya addressed the same issue during the 1977 Synod in Rome. Speaking on behalf of the bishops of central and eastern Africa, Cardinal Otunga firmly rejected the older missionary approaches in which the African religious and cultural heritage, when not completely ignored, was seen only as a *"preparatio evangelii"* that could be set aside once the work of evangelization had begun. He argued instead for the "new and dynamic image" of the "seeds of the Word" already present in Africa's traditional ways of being human and religious. "African culture," said the Cardinal, "possesses seeds that can produce flowers that have never been seen before."[33] This was a reaffirmation of the position taken by the same group of bishops at the previous Synod in 1974 when they urged "the necessity of fostering the particular incarnation of Christianity in each country, in accordance with the genius and talents of each culture, so that 'a thousand flowers may bloom in God's garden.'"[34]

These bishops, some seventy in number, declared unambiguously that "Christian life in Africa was insufficiently incarnated in African ways, customs and traditions." In their collective judgment, the Christian life was "very often lived merely at the surface without any real link of continuity with the genuine values of traditional religions." For them, moreover, "the so-called theology of adaptation was completely out of date." Instead, they argued for the adoption of "the theology of incarnation," with special respect for "the fact of religious pluralism."[35]

It was not only the African bishops who insisted upon the principle of incarnation. During the 1977 Synod many other participants were equally emphatic. The bishops of Asia, for example, jointly affirmed their solidarity with their African colleagues in these clear and succinct terms:

> The local church...is a church incarnate in the people. It is native, springing out of the local culture, with a reverence for ancient customs and traditions, speaking the local languages, dressed in local clothing, expressing immortal truths in the language that the common people can understand and love. The church must be local in its songs, in its way of life. As God became one of us—to make us his own—his church in Asia must be Asian, like the Asians in all things except sin.[36]

In 1979, I went searching for some of these rhetorical flowers mentioned at the synods in Rome, but not yet blooming in God's garden. As a Walsh-Price Fellow of the Catholic Foreign Mission Society of America (Maryknoll), I visited thirty-two mission stations scattered throughout the vast arid regions of Kenya. I interviewed, at length and in depth, dozens of missionaries, catechists and newly evangelized people.[37] These mission stations were chosen for my study because they served a variety of ethnic groups relatively untouched by the westernizing influences of the colonial period in Africa, and because most of the missionaries had arrived on the scene only since the end of Vatican Council II. In such places one might have expected to find, thanks to a renewed application of the incarnational principle, fresh and abundant expressions of African Christianity: not more drab copies of the western religious experience. But the "flowers that have never been seen before" in the church were hardly visible, aside from some scarce and precious buds here and there.

ETHNOCENTRISM AND PUSILLANIMITY

The scarcity of authentically African flowers blooming in the church's garden cannot now be due to ignorance on the part of missionaries and the local pastoral clergy in Africa. Nor would I attribute this to some alleged disobedience by these ministers. Indeed, increasing numbers of the younger and better educated clergy, especially among those who have completed advanced studies in theology or in the social sciences, are keenly interested in the possibility of a thoroughgoing Africanization of Christianity in Africa. Too many of them, however, despite the encouragement provided by a handful of senior African bishops, seem reluctant to take the risks inevitably entailed in the appropriate promotion of such a radically new orientation.

The general failure to apply earnestly and systematically the incarnational principle is certainly due in some measure today, as in the past, to a congenital and chronic ethnocentrism at the higher levels of ecclesiastical management. This point is made in Karl Rahner's rhetorical question:

> Do not the Roman Congregations still have the mentality of a centralized bureaucracy which thinks it knows best what serves the kingdom of God and the salvation of souls throughout the world, and in such decisions takes the mentality of Rome or Italy in a frighteningly naive way as a self-evident standard?[38]

More than anything else, however, the persisting failure to incarnate the Christian faith in African cultural worlds, may be due to a fear of innovation at the grassroots level. These are the fears mentioned by Pedro Arrupe when, as the Jesuit Superior General, he addressed the 1977 Synod of Bishops in Rome. Father Arrupe vigorously repudiated the widespread practice of "imposing upon people with cultures of their own certain foreign cultural patterns as the unique possibility for expressing the faith and the way to live it." Against this ethnocentrism and "the fears that arise to block inculturation completely or to diminish it," Arrupe reminded the assembly that our unique savior "saves only what he assumes." So, "it is needful...that all cultures be assumed by Christ; or, in other words, that all peoples be assumed by Christ through their own cultures," because faith never exists unless it is incarnated, for it is a way of life."[39]

It follows that Christ should assume into his body, which is the church, all cultures, purifying them "without destroying them." To those who "feel threatened by new or different expressions of faith, expressions that might possibly contradict what we (Europeans) have formulated and put into practice up to now," Arrupe says that "real pluralism is the most profound unity," and the present "crisis of unity in many cases is due to insufficient pluralism which fails to provide the satisfaction of expressing and living one's faith in conformity with one's own culture."[40] So it is, because all human beings are creatures of culture, always in need of some concrete cultural context as their own humanizing way of life within its own limited time-frame. Without some such matrix, one is acutely in danger of being reduced by the forces of anomie to "howling animality."[41] This danger is exemplified in contemporary history by the breakdown of cultures and the disintegration of social order in times of war or violent revolution.

There are other good reasons for allowing Christian communities everywhere to find their own new ways of self- expression in the varied terms of humankind's multiple cultural systems. Many of the church's doctrinal formulas, laws, social structures, styles and religious ceremonies—borrowed initially from Mediterranean cultures—no longer speak to the minds and hearts of people even in Europe and North America. These cultural "vessels of clay," as Avery Dulles calls them, were originally "intended to preserve, describe and transmit the gospel itself," but they have become "obsolete." Father Dulles' next line is especially relevant to the Christian communities of Africa today: "New doctrines, institutions, and ceremonies must be devised, not in order to replace the gospel, but to keep it alive and bring it to bear on the problems of the present age."[42] There is an urgent need to celebrate the Christian belief that God's re-creating love has been operative always and everywhere through the cultures of all peoples. Symbols capable of containing and communicating this belief can be found in African traditional religions.

We all know, anyway, what we should be doing in obedience to the directives of Vatican II, but for various reasons we dare not. What is lacking is courage in the face of ecclesiastical bureaucrats who too readily assume—while forgetting some of the more embarrassing lessons of church history—that the advocates of change, more than the defenders of the *status quo,* are apt to compromise the mission of the church among the nations. Still, the "fears" noted by Father Arrupe are understandable. The way of incarnation has been known to entail the crucifixion of a person daring to promote a different consciousness likely to usher in a new age.

RESOCIALIZATION CONTINUES

A frequently recited excuse for the non-implementation of the principle of inculturation is the feeble argument that only the African clergy are capable of incarnating the faith in their own cultural worlds. So the whole issue is deferred indefinitely, as the local clergy, far from being prepared by their clerical training for the inculturation challenge ahead of them, are still being intensively resocialized into imitation Euro-Americans. This is done through the universally standardized seminary system starting at secondary school level. The demands of this system make it virtually impossible for seminarians to immerse themselves deeply in their indigenous cultural worlds. So they are ordinarily unable to reach an appreciation of their own cultures equal in depth to that of their traditionally educated, but relatively less schooled, siblings. With every effort being made for many years to transform these seminarians into carbon copies of conventional western clergymen, it is neither fair nor honest to expect them to be the agents of inculturation at some time in the remote future. Did St. Paul and his associates first turn their new Christians and church leaders into imitation Jews with a view to their subsequently inculturating the faith in Greco-Roman cultural systems?

Among the tragic consequences of the current seminary system in Africa is the extent to which the indigenous clergy are apt to be alienated from their own cultural heritage. Some are notably uninterested in the religious and artistic traditions of their own people. Their resocialization experience into the invading culture and their encasement in a clerical subculture shaped by neo-scholasticism and legalism, has led to a situation in which the principle of inculturation can hardly be discussed, much less implemented.

Add to this the scramble for African "vocations" to fill the gaps in the declining religious orders, congregations and societies of Europe and North America. These organizations, with their archaic European models and molds for reshaping Africans, do even more than regular seminaries to confound or negate the original sociocultural and psychological identity of their African aspirants.[43] Unlike the earlier religious-missionaries in Africa, the recently arrived religious vocation "formaters" have plenty of money for the purchase of new cars and for erecting ample residences around the city of Nairobi in Kenya. These "houses of formation" are apt readily to attract the attention of young Africans anxious for higher educational opportunities and respected professional positions in a competitive world where these advantages are very hard to come by.

Yes, vocations seem plentiful in parts of Africa. It is no secret, nor is it a matter of shame, that young people from economically disadvantaged populations are, more than others, attracted to the religious life. Historically, this has been the case in countries of the north as well as the south. In some cases, however, one may wonder what the vow of poverty means to young men and women striving with all their energies and skills to find their way up and out of the grinding poverty and oppression so often characterizing the economic plight of African majorities these days. It even appears sometimes that priests belonging to religious orders enjoy greater economic security and more comfortable life-styles than the diocesan clergy.

Even more problematical is the alien image projected by these European and North American organizations. Are they not reinforcing the impression that Christianity itself is something left over from colonialism? In any event, it is hard to see how these religious orders, congregations and societies, with their vast accumulations of European cultural baggage— baroque styles, bourgeois mores, medieval symbols, rites, myths, gestures, rules, arts, concepts, customs and costumes—can help the church in Africa to overcome its congenital and chronic foreignness. The question addressed by Pope Paul VI in 1975 to six cardinals and forty bishops from Africa and Madagascar is germane:

> Does the Church in Africa retain a certain Christian religious
> form that was brought in from the outside and that makes her, as
> it were, a stranger and a pilgrim among her own people?[44]

How do the various "formation programs," historically dated and cul-ture-specific as they are, help with the great task of inculturation? This objective is hardly served by resocializing young Africans in these borrowed ways, as though African traditions lacked the spiritual resources and the cre-ativity needed for structuring the religious commitments of Africans. Saul's panoply was, for David, only an impediment, in part comical, in part omi-nous, inviting a debacle. Is this what the seminaries and "houses of forma-tion" are for young Christians in Africa?

MORE RATIONALIZATIONS

Another argument sometimes adduced for doing nothing to promote the cultural catholicity of the church in Africa is the facile assertion that African cultures are archaic and vanishing under the impact of westernizing modernity. These cultures, now regarded as obsolescent by some western and westernized scholars, used to be called "savage" or "primitive." All such pejorative judgments arise, according to Evan M. Zuesse, from western per-ceptions shaped by a deep and misleading paradigm defending western feel-ings of superiority against any possibility of eclipse by other cultures. "To suppose that these cultures have in their traditional forms both the avenues and the power to deal with problems of nationalization, industrialism, and the scientific method is to pose a real challenge to our own lives."[45]—to our western ways of dealing with these features of modernity. Likewise, to suppose that Christianity's self-expression might be enriched and clarified through traditional African symbol systems is to raise disturbing questions about the adequacy of the religious experiences and expressions of western peoples. Under the lid of colonialism such questions were hardly thinkable. Even now these issues are apt to be considered too threatening to be formulated in unambiguous terms.

It is not surprising, therefore, that many Africans, profoundly resocialized through the churches, schools and universities of the colonial period, have been "westernized" or "modernized." This was done for the benefit of the colonizing powers, and at a great personal and social cost to Africans. By internalizing the pejorative judgments of their western teachers and preachers, these Africans promoted the west's social, cultural, religious and economic hegemony, while at the same time denigrating their own heritage.[46] This misdirected loyalty had the effect of inhibiting, if not totally precluding, any likelihood of authentically African cultural systems of humanism and social order (ethics, law, religion, art, etc.) meeting the new needs of African peoples. Among the consequences of this disintegrative process, depriving people of their traditional ethical and religious systems, is a growing amorality and religious indifference among African elites, even an emerging atheism in practice. It is no secret that some African populations have been led, more often than not under the banner of "progress" or "modernity," to the brink of anomie, while others have already fallen into a state of total chaos.

So it has been uncritically assumed by many educated people that technological commercialism, and the new acquisitiveness driven by advertising and television "entertainment," will eventually yield a homogeneous culture of modernity. For example, the "now-generation" everywhere loves Coca Cola! A concomitant illusion is that only a Euro-American version of Christianity, with a few token adaptations, is compatible with "progress." This is a view sometimes urged by expatriates living in African countries. It is also a "common sense" opinion held by some Africans in the so-called "progressive," "advanced" or "modern" sectors. These sectors generally consist of people who have been extensively resocialized. Many of them are remote from, and sometimes ashamed of, their own cultural roots. Moreover, these people are apt to belong to the affluent elite usually living in large cities where government services and the national wealth are concentrated, often ostentatiously, for their benefit. Indeed, these population segments, frequently using European instead of African languages, may well be developing new subcultures which must also be taken seriously by the churches.

Relative to the masses of disadvantaged and dispossessed Africans with their extraordinarily high population growth rates, however, the advantaged elite are numerically much less significant than they appear to be. Their demise is even predictable in some countries, and a fact of history in some others. It is well known, moreover, that urban populations, with better opportunities for schooling and less inhibited by traditional restraints, are particularly at risk from AIDS which is now endemic in some countries. Most Africans, on the other hand, still live in rural areas where both quality schooling of a modernizing type and health services are either absent or declining, while traditional influences are not only strong, but may even be increasing, because the ways of modernity hardly meet the basic needs of these vast majorities. According to some very grim estimates by United Nations demographers, about one out of every three Africans may be undernourished, while several countries have under-five mortality rates in the area of 300 out of 1,000 live births. All reasonable predictions are that for most people in Africa things will get worse economically before they get better, and much worse demographically because of AIDS. Even in the cities of Africa, most of the inhabitants belong to the economically disadvantaged classes. They usually cluster together in ethnic enclaves where, in spite of modernity's vulgar incursions, their respective cultural systems are still vibrant.

TRADITIONS STILL ALIVE

African cultures, even under the costly clothing of modernity, still show signs of vitality and varying degrees of relevance for the self-understanding of countless millions of people. Otherwise, what is the meaning of all the comments of African church leaders cited above? Why, otherwise, would they be so insistent upon the cultural Africanization of the church? For evidence of the long-term viability of traditional African religions, in spite of enormous foreign pressures working systematically against them, we need only look at the surviving religious systems of the Yoruba and Igbo people even outside their own homelands in Nigeria. Their pantheons and rituals, carried from West Africa to Brazil and the Caribbean countries generations ago by enslaved populations, are still dynamic elements in the religious celebrations of these regions.[47] Indeed, these African structures are flourishing both as separate religions and in mixed forms with the Christianity of Iberian colonialism.

If African ways of being religious have retained their vibrancy during generations of captivity in foreign lands, then we may expect them also to be quite alive, even if well hidden, in their homelands today. This point, so often overlooked by churchmen in Africa, is illustrated by the research of the Nigerian theologian Elochukwu Uzukwu: "Right from the beginning of missionary evangelism in Igboland (1854) to the period of pacification (1901–1910), the Igbo world view has braved the challenge and attacks of the Western world view (propagated by Christianity through the educational system completely dominated by missionaries)."[48] Schools, used for evangelizing their impressionable audiences, resembled nothing so much as factories mass-producing new Christians. This type of evangelism often consisted in little more than memorizing translated prayers, doctrinal formulas, biblical texts, foreign songs and alien laws—with the fear of punishment as the motive force. This yielded large numbers of church-goers. But it also amounted to, at least tacitly, a systematic denigrating of the children's immemorial cultural heritage.

Aside from this moral coercion in schools, Uzukwu grants the probability that many people freely accepted the worldview introduced by missionaries, because they found it more satisfying than their own Igbo traditions. It should be added that, in spite of all the psycho-social consequences of the persistent monoculturalism noted in this book, authentic Christians, both anonymous and named, may be found everywhere in Africa. After all, God's grace is more powerful than the cultural obtuseness of missionary and ecclesiastical officialdom combined.

Nevertheless, Father Uzukwu's study of "the contradictory life of a great number of Igbo Christians, since the earliest times of conversion to the contemporary period, testifies eloquently to the preference or, perhaps, attraction of the traditional world view in the search for equilibrium." Much evidence may be cited in support of this thesis. There are, for example, many lapsed Christians now returning to their traditional religion. Nor is it unusual for "practicing" Christians to offer traditional sacrifices to secure fecundity, healing, appeasement of malignant spirits, or to break pacts made with persons since deceased and now considered negative influences. Another "very widespread practice" is the keeping or wearing of "protective medicines....It is an open secret that, among those who consult diviners/doctors today, Christians are in the majority."[49] Similar evidence of religious dualism, illustrating Christianity's unintegrated and extrinsic character, may be found throughout sub-Saharan Africa.

Careful research among almost any of Africa's ethnic-culture groups, however Christianized and modernized, is bound to reveal the perduring and meaningful presence of the people's religious and ethical traditions, at least in their more important symbol systems. These are apt to be found functioning side by side with the foreign systems introduced during the colonial period. A widespread example of this is the presence of two different conceptualizations and institutionalizations of the man-woman relationship called marriage. Both the traditional African systems and those from the north may be found operating separately in the same society, and in ways that are, if not always complementary, at least compatible or mutually tolerable.[50] But in situations of conflict, which are not uncommon, the one that counts ultimately in the sight of the people is the traditional system. Without that cultural support, an African marriage tends to be very fragile.

Further examples of dual cultural systems operating in the same area are the varied ways different peoples have developed for coping with death. Africa's traditional systems, often overlooked by ecclesiastical officials, and sometimes hidden from them, may be more meaningful to the people than the standard Euro-American funeral rites used in the churches of Africa. An inquiry into the dual mortuary rites of the Chagga people living on the slopes of Mt. Kilimanjaro in northern Tanzania would be particularly interesting. Thanks to the early German colonial interventions, almost all of these people are either Catholics or Lutherans. For generations, they have listened to missionaries and local pastors condemning their "pagan" cultural practices, even referring to the non-Christians among them as *washenzi,* a Swahili term of contempt, roughly equivalent to "heathens" or "barbarians." Nevertheless, some time after the Christian obsequies in church, all the family members show up elsewhere for the traditional rites. Even relatives, who are priests, do what the traditional rites require (e.g., heads shaved in a specified style).

So, the challenge of inculturation remains unavoidable. To ascertain in more detail just what this might entail, the following chapter presents a general introduction to the major themes and elements constituting one particular African traditional religion which is certainly not archaic. The fourth chapter raises some specific questions to be faced by church functionaries with the imagination and courage demanded by Christianity's primordial principle of incarnation.

III

An African Traditional Religion (Maasai)

To understand the nature of revealed religion, we have to understand the nature of the so-called natural religion, for nothing could have been revealed about anything if men (and women) had not already had an idea about the thing. Or rather, perhaps we should say that the dichotomy between natural and revealed religion is false...for there is a good sense in which it may be said that all religions are religions of revelation....We might ponder the words of St. Augustine: "What is now called Christian religion has existed among the ancients, and is not absent from the beginning of the human race, until Christ came in the flesh; from which time the true religion, which existed already, was called Christian."   —E.E. Evans-Pritchard[1]

The lines quoted above, from his 1965 book on primal religions, suggest that Oxford University's famous professor of anthropology had been paying attention to the proceedings of the Second Vatican Council as it prepared the ground for a radically new attitude toward non-Christian religions. As divine grace presupposes nature, so any revelation from God presupposes the mundane experience of persons within a humanly created and historically conditioned cultural context. Referring to the traditional religious component in an African culture, Eboussi Boulaga says "it was being born, living and dying in the most empirical manner that ever could be that furnished the framework, the matter and the experience of God's sacramental and sovereign immanence."[2]

The notes presented in the following pages on prayer, God, holiness, blessings, curses, fertility and ritual slaughtering ("sacrifice"?) are derived from codes containing the immemorial religious experience of the Maasai peoples inhabiting the great game-filled plains on both sides of the Kenya-Tanzania border in East Africa just below the equator. By reflecting on the dynamic meanings communicated through the common and recurring uses of these condensed forms of religious experience, an opening may be found into the riches of the Maasai cultural world. Also a more positive appreciation of their traditional religion may be gained when this is seen as a culturally integrated system for commemorating and celebrating God's gift of life. Their religion, no less than any other authentic religious system, is a creation of the analogical imagination of the people in a world inundated with grace.

The religious experience of the Maasai, as a preliterate people, is not recorded in holy books. It is, however, contained in the memory of the people, and it is repeatedly expressed through their traditional symbols, myths, rituals, attitudes and practices. These amount to a living religion, a dynamic symbol system of communication, permeating their whole cultural world. Divine revelation is not confined exclusively to what is indicated in the Bible, nor are Judeo-Christian religious practices the only proper ways of responding to God's self-communication which is always and everywhere mediated to all peoples in the terms of their respective historico-cultural situations. So, Christians everywhere may have something to learn from the divine revelations (good news) reflected in the expressions and celebrations of African traditional religions.

MAASAI RELIGION

There is no word for religion as such in the traditional language of the Maasai of Kenya and Tanzania.[3] But these subsistence pastoralists—known among themselves as *Ilmaasai, Ilparakuyu,* and *Isampur*—have common cultural experiences that are clearly religious in their ability to renew the hope of the people, and sustain them spiritually, generation after generation. This is done successfully in the face of the perplexities, pains, anxieties and expectations of the human sojourn in some of Africa's less hospitable bioclimatic regions, and under precarious economic conditions.

The immemorial religious experiences of the pastoral Maasai are encoded in stories and symbols serving as templates for community coherence, continuity, courage, hope and joy. These experiences are reactivated significantly in ritual celebrations reaffirming consciously and emotionally the confidence of the peoples in the existing order of reality. Here we offer in a summary manner some notes and reflections on the principal religious themes encoded in some of the symbols, myths and rituals which constitute an integral and pervasive component of Maasai culture. But these few pages amount to no more than a sample of the rich religious symbolism permeating the lives of these people, informing, shaping and coloring their cultural ethos, social structures, spirituality, piety, mores, ethics and worldview.

PRAYING TO GOD

If religion is understood as a matter of praying to a deity, then the Maasai are quite religious. Prayer is a notable feature of daily life in their traditional society. Here the average adult probably prays more frequently than most Christians. Even the young unmarried men follow a regular regimen of prayer. The Maasai have many prayer forms, some long and some short, but all are very adaptable to different occasions, allowing also for individual creativity and spontaneity. An analysis of their prayers provides a vantage point for appreciating the people's values, and their perception of the ultimate transcendent reality called God.

The Maasai address the divinity directly with a great variety of names which are metaphorical masks for the incomprehensible ground of all reality, the inscrutable mystery of life behind the visible universe. In terms of the historico-cultural experience of the people, the names are meaningful and disclosive to those "who have ears to hear." The address is sometimes formal but often it is personal and even familiar in tone. The most prominent name for the deity is *Enkai*, literally translated as "Originator."[4] From the context of the prayers it is evident that Enkai is perceived as unique and universal, immanent and transcendent, powerful and righteous, yet personal and helpful in relation to humankind.[5]

The people say that *Enkai* is neither male nor female, although the gender of this word is feminine. They insist that "He," or "She," or "It," is not comparable to a man, a woman, or a thing, while still being somehow like humankind, *oltungani*.[6] It is noteworthy that in this strictly patriarchal society God should be addressed more often than not in the feminine gender. On the analogy of the mothering role of women in Maasai society, the feminine prefix probably provides a reverential connotation respecting the originating sources of life and the tender nurturing that life requires.

In one of the traditional Maasai myths about how things were in the beginning, thus how things really are even now, the first human being is called *Naiterukop*. Literally this means "She who begins the earth," or "the beginner of the world," or "the first one on earth."[7] Because of the tone used, this name does not refer explicitly to the divinity. However, from the context of the unfolding story, although the various versions may be somewhat confused or embellished by the narrator, the reference is to the beginning of the whole human enterprise on earth, *enkop*, in all its ethnic and cultural diversity. The use of the feminine singular relative prefix *na* with the verb stem "begin," *iter*, might be taken as an allusion to the Originator, *Enkai*, as She who begins or originates. It does seem appropriate, in any case, to think of the divinity as She. All our lives begin in and through womanhood.

Various other anthropomorphic images, both masculine and feminine, occur frequently in Maasai prayers. In light of the specifically male function of protecting the herds and flocks against predators, *Enkai* may be seen as a strong and steady guardian: "(Our) shepherd night and day."[8] In the very same prayer, however, *Enkai* may be pictured in an exclusively female role, as the people call upon her to "keep us in your stomach...carry us on your back...tie us around your arm like a bracelet...place us in the whiteness of your womb and do not take us out again." All such prayers are typically concluded with formulas like this: "and *Enkai* said, 'all right'"; or simply the feminine vocative term "Oh God," *Naai*.[9]

Some of the other common metaphors used for the divinity are apt to be immediately intelligible only to people experientially immersed in the cultural world of the Maasai. *Enkai* may be addressed, for example, as "One who puts in and takes out," "Many colored," "Grayish-blue stomach," "My thundering one," "My one of newly formed grass," "My splendor of the morning," "My red light of dawn," "One who separates the paths," "Far one and near one," "My bright star," "One who brings to life," "My feathered one," (any hen with chicks, or an ostrich).[10]

The last title, speaking of the divinity in avian imagery, suggests transcendence, fertility and mothering. This also resonates with the ancient religious symbolism of birds and feathers found in many different religions. Birds and feathers also feature prominently in the headdress of Maasai boys during their ritual passage into adulthood. Such imagery, even that of the hen, is used also in the Bible: "I call upon you, God...hide me in the shade of your wings" (Ps 17:8); and "...as the hen gathers her brood under her wings" (Mt 23:37). There is also the symbol of the Holy Spirit as a dove (John 1:32). Alluding to Genesis (1:2), G. M. Hopkins wrote of the Spirit who "over the bent world broods with warm breast and ah! bright wings."

As a more comprehensive, yet cognate, metaphor for the divinity, the Maasai occasionally use the word *enkai* for "sky." It is hard to think of a more awesome symbol for the Originator of everything, the One who oversees, embraces and cares for all. "My God," the people pray, "you are surrounded by stars, with the moon at your navel; you last forever."[11] What is symbolized here is surely that same ultimate horizon of hope which Jews, Muslims and Christians haltingly name *Yahweh* or *Elohim* or *Allah,* or "God" (a term derived from pre-Christian Teutonic religious experience).

Again, the special term *Enkai* is sometimes used also for "rain" which obviously has an originating function, producing the vegetation without which the livestock, and consequently the people, could not survive in the marginal lands inhabited by the Maasai. With such adequate symbols and rich metaphors speaking directly to the daily experience of the people, the Maasai feel no need to reduce their consciousness of the holy mystery of reality to abstract concepts and philosophical categories (e.g., the Totally Other or Absolute Being). Instead of formulating dogmas and imposing laws, they prefer to express their religious experience joyously in song and dance, solidarity and festivity.[12] The various connotations of the word *Enkai* suggest, moreover, the extent to which the authentic religious experience of the people is reflected throughout their culture. As with Jews and Christians, God is an unfathomable mystery, "Many Colored" (*Parmuain*), who can hardly be named precisely, much less pictured exactly. But *Enkai* is no changeless Aristotelian "thought thinking itself." She is more like the Hebrew divinity encountering people through historical events.

THE VENERABLE ELDERS

The venerable elders are gentlemen of the most senior age groups. These elders—currently of the age groups called *Iltareto, Ilterito, Ilnyangusi, Iseuri*—are considered to be much wiser and holier than most of today's younger Maasai who are their children, grandchildren and great-grandchildren. Having been around much longer (for more or less 50 to 90 years), the elders are more experienced anyway, hence apt to be wiser, at least in their corporate deliberations and decisions. As the Maasai say, "We begin by being foolish and we become wise by experience."[13] Their longevity also suggests that they may be more esteemed by "Her who puts in and takes out." The elders with many children are themselves, obviously, much blessed by *Enkai* who has prolonged their lives and made them so productive. A long and fruitful life suggests holiness, *esinyatisho*. Maasai society is a gerontoc-racy,[14] deriving its legitimacy both from the common sense of the people and from their perception of the divinity's relationship to humankind.

"Between God and the entire Maasai people," as they themselves say, "there is unity."[15] The venerable elders are a part standing representatively for the whole people. Moreover, the elders are closer to all the Maasai who went before into the ground and "are no longer around," especially those deceased elders who had wisely guided the people of previous generations in their historical sojourn. The sense of corporate unity and continuity is strong. But Maasai respect for their progenitors does not amount to any kind of so-called "ancestor worship." Respect, awe and fear associated with the venera-ble elders, hence their authority, derives from the proximity of these patri-archs to *Enkai* who is both far and near, while perennially bringing life and separating the paths.

The essential social function of these elders is to discern the right order of things, and to guide their society along the path of right order and truth: "to seek the right order."[16] This is done by looking back at how things were, in relation to how things are now, and how they should be. This is not done by individuals in isolation; it is a collective exercise involving much discus-sion, while reaching for consensus. The elders thus function as the protectors of the traditional culture which has enabled the people not only to survive but to become what they have been in the best of times, to establish what they should be now, and to promote what they should become in the future. As a part of the Maasai community, standing for the whole people, these elders appear also to have, collectively, a quasi-priestly role of intercession; their formal prayers together are considered to be particularly efficacious. Indeed, every mature Maasai has ready examples to illustrate this efficacy: e.g., how the ritual prayers of the elders brought rain during a time of drought, or how so-and-so was cured after a prayerful anointing by the hands of the local elders.

Because of the respect they enjoy, the venerable elders are able to maintain the community's sense of right order, balance and integrity in the face of external threats and natural disasters auguring anomie and chaos. Thus the younger Maasai, thanks to their senior guardians, are socialized and oriented in ways that enable them to make sense out of the events impinging upon their lives. Through their confidence in the wisdom and holiness of the venerable elders, as a social institution, each individual Maasai is enabled to identify his or her role, and to feel at home, in the total context of the Maasai cultural world. Anxieties are tamed by plausible explanations for everything, as order and meaning are maintained not only objectively by institutional structures (e.g., the stratified age groups and differentiation of responsibilities), but also subjectively as the consciousness of individuals is shaped by the comprehensive socialization process with its historically linear rites of passage from birth to death, from immaturity to a fullness of fruitful living with a memorable legacy for future generations.

BLESSINGS

To bless, *amayian*, is a formal way of praying which belongs commonly and most appropriately, but not exclusively, to the venerable elders of Maasai society. Ordinary prayers are addressed to God; but blessings look directly to the persons or objects being blessed. Here, for example, are some wishful blessings:[17] "Let the Kisonko people be Maasai with you." "Make the Kaputie people milk their breasts and udders, in the evening and in the morning." "Make something of all of us." "Say, let it be sweet (the matter at hand)." To each invocation the typical response by those present is "Oh God," *Naai*. Another blessing, concerned with the safety of a person going on a long safari, would consist of a series of invocations like these: "Go to places far and wide, and may God be with you." "Go, honor your forebears, and come back with their sweetest of honeys." "Go then, but respect your father and mother, then God will be with you."

The act of blessing, *emayianata*, frequently entails, together with invocations, some modest ritual gestures, such as a spray of spittle, or a symbolic binding with blades of grass. Blessings supported by spittings, *inkamulak*, are efficacious; they are fully expected to have divine concurrence, and thus accomplish what they proclaim. Spittle gives life to words and expectations. Combined with the breathing out of words, spittle becomes a very efficacious symbol of life communicated from one person to another. Such symbols, arising from the inner depths of respected persons, who themselves are obviously blessed by God with long life and fecundity, clearly participate in what they signify. That which is signified is thus communicated through sound and water.

The wetness of nature and of living human beings is manifestly productive, fruitful, fecund, life-giving. So, any respected persons may be asked to spray a little spittle over children as a blessing. Close friends may sometimes spit into their hands just before shaking hands after a long absence. There is also the related symbol of kissing, used commonly among the Maasai. All such gestures have their complex rules, not always appreciated by outsiders, respecting the appropriate times, places and persons.

Blessings enhanced with spittle can be more or less elaborate, depending largely upon the customary requirements of the occasion. But these rituals have a casual and spontaneous character about them. It is almost as though the rite were being invented, step-by-step, by the participants as they move along from one gesture to another. Maasai rituals are not artistic theatrics, much less magical legalisms. They are significant ways of approaching or encountering the inner realities of life, existence, history, destiny, flesh and finitude. The full meaning of these realities is not seen on the level of empirical experience and functionality, but on another level of human experience encoded in the traditional cultural symbols of the people. The really real is approached, however, according to a general pattern with formal features and common elements.

The more solemn blessings by a group of venerable elders are done in the presence of a representative segment of the local Maasai community. Wetness is a central theme, often consisting of milk and honey in the form of mead. These elements are mixed sometimes with water and special "medicines" in a calabash. These liquids of life are taken into the mouths of those imparting the blessings, whence they are sprayed out on the persons or objects being blessed. The liquid may also be dispensed from a calabash with its opening partly blocked by grass, so the fluid can be sprinkled out as droplets. A handful of green grass, with its own life-giving significance, may also be used in the manner of the aspergillum used in the Catholic rite of sprinkling holy water as a sign of blessing.

A person being blessed sits on a stool in the center of a circle of elders. The recipient is presented with green grass to be held in the left hand (the right hand is for weapons) and some grass is placed on the head. Four chosen elders encircle the subject clockwise and four others counterclockwise, spitting out their blessing and sprinkling the symbolic fluids of life. All the while there is a stream of invocations, numerous and solemn, recited by the leader. Some examples:[18] "Tread (the grass) that is green." "Yours will be sweetness." "May the green grass love you." "Let the wind love you." "Let the moon love you." "May God open roads for you." Each of these is followed by the usual response of all present, "Oh God."

Wetness, in the varied ritual uses of water, is universally one of the richest of religious symbols. Spittle, we may recall, was used by Jesus in healing rites (Mark 7:33; 8:23; John 9:6). Until late in this century, it was also used in the Catholic rite of baptism. The ritual immersion of initiates in flowing waters is much older and more widespread than the Judeo-Christian practice of baptism, which rational legalism in much of the western world has reduced to the pouring of a few drops of water on the heads of new

Christians. Water signifies many realities beyond the empirical level of experience. Cleaning, purifying, refreshing, renewing, fecundity, generation, regeneration, chaos and destruction are some of the meanings, or layers of meaning, that wetness has for humankind. In the bio-climatic regions inhabited by Africa's subsistent pastoralists like the Maasai, permanent water sources are scarce; rainfall patterns are erratic and unreliable. Here wetness is profoundly meaningful in the lives of the people. It is one of their most common life-related symbols.

CURSES

Respect, *enkanyit*, is the central social virtue of Maasai society. This word connotes reverence, piety, obedience, right behavior and good manners.[19] *Enkanyit* is thus the dynamic element in the Maasai system of social control, having been drilled into the people during all the stages of growth from childhood to elderhood, and especially through the formal rites of passage. This system's principal sanctions are public opinion and the ability of the venerable elders (also all parents) to threaten with curses anyone persistently guilty of seriously deviant behavior which might damage "right order." For example, a son's contumacious disobedience to his father might occasion a curse. Given the traditional absence of coercion in the form of police, prisons and capital punishment—together with the relatively rare occurrence of such crimes as calumny, detraction, theft, rape and murder—the maintenance of "right order" through the ideal of respect and the threat of curses has worked well. Curses in the Maasai social context may be seen as positive, even if only occasionally used and rarely lethal. Certain crimes, such as the killing of a Maasai or any woman, entail an automatic curse upon the culprit.

Of course, there are some individuals inclined to use the curse for base motives such as revenge or envy. In doing so, however, they expose themselves to the danger of an equivalent backlash from their own mischief. The curse, usually amounting to only the threat of a curse, is considered socially constructive and appropriate. It is the opposite side of blessings, having the same source and purpose: the promotion of "right order" for the good of all.

The imposition of curses, and especially their removal, involve some ritual actions. The chief spokesman, *olaiguenani,* of an age group, for example, has the power, which is almost never used, to lay a curse on all his constituents. He could do this symbolically by vigorously casting to the ground his special symbol of authority, his staff of office, an ebony club, *okiuka*. To curse an individual of his age group, the spokesman may remove from his dark blue necklace one bead, casting it away while naming the accursed individual represented by that bead. The necklace consists of a bead for each of the group members represented by the spokesman as a corporate personality, a part standing for the whole.

The removal of curses usually involves more elaborate gestures suggesting blessings in reverse, and sometimes using analogous binding actions to render the curse significantly ineffectual. These are all very powerful ways of delivering messages of disapproval (comparable to ecclesiastical censures) and of conditioned acceptance back into the community (excommunications lifted). These various actions are intended only for the promotion and maintenance of "right order." The most powerful instrument required for the removal of certain curses is the ritual slaughtering of animals.

RITUAL SLAUGHTERING

As part of their culturally invented educational and humanizing processes (socialization or enculturation), endowing persons with their self-understanding and social identity, all peoples have their own rites of passage. The numerous Maasai rites of passage are always associated with prayerful invocations, multiple blessings, and a ritual slaughtering, *empolosare,* or *empolosata,* of choice animals. For major ceremonies the usual choice is a black ox with a white stomach and no blemish. Each of these religious enactments is clearly a joyous celebration of life. But these occasions are marked by solemnity as well as festivity.

Ritual slaughtering differs in a number of ways from the ordinary killing of animals just for eating. On special ceremonial occasions (e.g., *eunoto*) the chosen black ox is first intoxicated with mead; songs are sung to it, and it is anointed from head to tail with "medicine."[20] The ritual slaughtering of the victim is done not with a knife, but by smothering. This method prevents any spilling of blood which is neatly drawn into the animal's dewlap and thus made available to the participants in the ritual. The blood is taken by them in a mixture of mead, milk and "medicine," *entasim,* prepared from roots, leaves and bark.[21] "Under certain circumstances, sacrifice is signaled to God by placing the stomach of the animal above the doorway of the owner's house, or placing its head before the ritual house or sanctuary."[22] On all occasions of ritual slaughtering a new fire is made by the ancient method of rubbing a firestick, *olpiron,* with one end in a groove on a board, *entoole.*

By doing this, a man (never a woman) "aims to start/begin a fire," *eipirua enkima*. Such an action is more than merely functional; it may also be seen as symbolizing the generation of new life.

Also on these occasions, the sacrificial victim is placed on its back, with the head pointing northeastward and the stomach (when the animal is on its side) facing north, *kopikop*. This is also a mortuary position for deceased persons. Presumably the face is looking toward the place where the Maasai people originated—probably in northern Kenya's Kerio valley south of Lake Turkana, if not further north in a place described only by the type of trees found there.[23] These are trees with nettles, *olooltamiyioo*, referring probably to the wild olive, respected for its excessive output of pollen for the production of new life; also prized as firewood and for its burning charcoal used for sterilizing the insides of calabashes (milk or mead containers). It is from some such place that the Maasai came in their historical migration, generally toward the south in their unending search for the "sweet land of milk and honey," *enkop namelok kule o enaisho.*

After the north, the ritually important direction is *oloosaen*, "it-of-the-beads," referring to the east, whence the resplendent sunrise symbolized by the multicolored beads commonly worn by Maasai women,[24] and of course by the women themselves who have so much to do with the arrival of new life. To the Maasai imagination, the beads reflect a splendor analogous to that of the rising sun as source of life and hope. From the same direction of the Indian Ocean come the cowrie shells greatly esteemed for decorative purposes, while symbolizing—in their shape, appearance and durability—everyone's original passage out of an originating chamber of fluid to a beautiful and lasting human life. Sunrise and sunset represent life and death, respectively. So, for some Maasai, the head of the sacrificial animal should be pointing north with the face and stomach looking eastward. This is also a human mortuary position. According to some informants, the face should be looking east and the head pointing south in the general direction of the historical movement of the Maasai from north to south.

On major ceremonial occasions, such as the rites of passage into stages of warriorhood and stages of elderhood—*eunoto* ("planting" the age group), *olngesher* ("grill" for roasting meat), *olkiteng loo lbaa* ("ox of the wounds")—specially designated cuts of roasted meat are eaten by the participants in a ritual manner. The brisket, *enkiyieu,* is particularly significant, as the center of life is within the chest. The divided hide of the victim is shared among the participants, each then wearing a ring or a bracelet fashioned from the hide. However, sacrificial rituals of purification after certain sins, *ingok*—for example, killing a Maasai or killing any woman—require that the slaughtered animal be left in the bush to be consumed by hyenas. Nor is the meat eaten when, in the face of some calamity such as drought or plague, the victim is offered to *Enkai;* then it is totally immolated in sacrificial flames, *olasar.*

In a number of other significant ways the slaughtered ox points to God and the corporate unity of the participants in the ritual. As a part standing for the whole, the participants represent the entire Maasai people in their historical journey through life's passages. Some of the invocations and acclamations used just before the ritual killing suggest that death is somehow a way to new life or its continuation.[25] It is clear, anyway, that the victim's flesh nourishes the participants, invigorating and sustaining them; even, in a symbolic sense, giving them life. This is reminiscent of the imagery of the seed that must die in the ground as a precondition for the production of new and more abundant life; it also recalls the ritual significance of Jesus' astonishing teaching about eating his flesh and drinking his blood as a way to eternal life in union with him (cf. John 6:53–58).

Such ceremonial slaughtering and eating are central not only to the major rites of passage but also to the periodic fertility rites of women and the prayer sessions of the elders asking for rain during the recurring drought years. The ritual is appropriately concluded with the immolation of all the remains, including the bones, in flames fed by a mixture of both green and dry grass sending up clouds of smoke into the sky, *enkai.* Where available, a sweet smelling weed is added to the burning grass, giving fragrance to the rising smoke.

Instead of trying to locate the essential meaning of the ritual slaughtering in some particular action—the killing of the victim, the eating of its flesh, the dividing of its hide, the multiple invocations and blessings, the burning of the remains—the whole complex of symbols and gestures may be seen as the "sacrifice," *empolosare* or *olasar.* The former term refers to the tearing or dividing of the meat and the hide to be shared by the participants. As *empolosata o lkiteng*, "passing through the ox," it also refers to pushing the middle finger through a hole in a piece of the victim's hide cut to serve as a ring to be worn by each of the participants in the ritual.[26] The latter term, *olasar*, refers to the ceremonial flame used for roasting the meat and immolating the remains.[27]

Rather than the offering of a victim to God in some type of propitiation, the ritual "passing through the ox" may be seen as a celebration of the gift of life from God. It may also be interpreted as a thanksgiving feast celebrating not only God's generosity but also the unity and survivability of the Maasai people. Every person's journey through life entails various kinds and series of "passing through" precarious avenues, valleys and waters. From the beginning, according to a well-known Maasai myth recounting the original event of divine benevolence toward humankind, God's gift of cattle enabled the Maasai to live as they have with a measure of security and prosperity in their semi-arid lands. Other peoples, according to the same myth, were given wild animals or vegetation as bases for their respective economies. But the subsistence of the Maasai is contingent upon the productivity of domestic livestock.

In the ritual sharing of a slaughtered animal's meat and hide (communion), the people's "link with God is intensified, as if it is the gift of life itself that is 'passed' through the ox, directly from God to the celebrants."[28] The communicants, as a part standing for the whole Maasai people, represent and reaffirm the people's original relationship with God. Not only that primal relationship but also the mutuality and unity of all the people are celebrated in feasting, singing and dancing together. The participants do symbolically, hence really in some measure, what the rite signifies, memorialize and celebrate. In their ritual reenactment, they make present again, in dramatic symbolism, the pristine Maasai experience of *Enkai's* benevolence and their unity with her. This religious consciousness is sustained perennially in the memory of the people, because of the retelling of the myth and its periodic ritualization in ways that are joyful and memorable. It is especially in the major rites of passage that the participants' present experience connects most significantly with the remembered experience of the whole people.

As with all ritual performances, the richness and depth of meaning are conveyed variously, and more or less successfully, by the symbols and gestures themselves, to the inhabitants of the Maasai "forest of symbols." The symbolic action, as a part of the reality standing for the whole relationship between God and the people, really does in some measure what it signifies, memorializes and celebrates. These prayerful ways of celebrating life and thanking God, especially in association with the rites of passage, reinforce the inherited identity and self-understanding of the people, providing them with powerful, pervasive and durable images, moods, attitudes, feelings, concepts and motivations; thus dramatically confirming for them the plausibility of their own traditional and existential system of coordinates which are, for them, transcendentally grounded and immanently operative.[29] Here we see how religion, as a component of culture, serves massively to maintain a people's sociocultural integrity and historical continuity; how also it helps to keep at bay the "primeval forces of darkness," the ever threatening social chaos that is "the oldest antagonist" of decency, beauty and holiness.[30]

FERTILITY RITES

While all Maasai religious enactments reflect a major concern with the origins and continuities of life, the women's fertility rites, *olamal,* express this most explicitly, reverently and intensively. In their historical context of high infant and child mortality rates, and in their labor-intensive subsistence economy, the bearing of children is the most obvious key not only to wealth and security but to human survival. The dominant social value in traditional Maasai families is children—many, healthy, much loved and well-behaved. Indeed, every newborn child is seen as a joyful sign of divine blessing upon the whole people. The care, attention and tenderness bestowed upon young children is a signal characteristic of Maasai society. The future of the Maasai people, and of humankind generally, obviously resides in children.[31]

Periodically during the wet season, on the initiative and under the direction of the local prophet/ritual expert, *oloiboni,* a large group of women, as a part standing for all in a particular area, participate in the ritual slaughtering, *empolosare,* of an ox. The fat of this animal is used for anointing the bodies of each of the women, also for oiling their sheepskin gowns. All the participants—each one wearing a bracelet and a necklace, *olkereti,* cut from the bark of the *oreteti* tree—dance and sing their way together to a holy place in the forest, chanting their prayers as they go, asking God to bless them with children. A commonly recurring chant is "God, I beg motherhood," *Enkai aomon entomono.*

When women band together, especially on these occasions, their ritual enactments are taken very seriously by the entire community. The processing women are given gifts at each village visited along the way. They must be respected, because their prayers "bear the promise of future life for the community as a whole."[32] The site of these ritual prayers is beneath a large and ancient tree, *oreteti,* which, when struck with a stick, yields a sweet tasting milky liquid. During their constant procession around the tree, the women continue chanting their prayers. They are doing what their mothers did before them in the same holy place; also their grandmothers and great grandmothers, from time immemorial.

The few men participating in the women's procession around the tree are in liminal garb similar to that of the women. Each carries a gourd of fresh cow's milk and a clump of green grass. They offer libations of fresh cow's milk sprinkled on the tree trunk, the grass serving as a kind of aspergillum. All the participants in this ritual, far from having any doubts about the Originator's positive response, are confident that many children will soon be born into their families. A deep sense of trust and hope becomes palpable through this ritual enactment. Even an outside observer is apt to be caught up vicariously in the religious experience of the actual participants. It is hard to believe that the hopeful chants of these numerous women are not heard high above the clouds in the blue sky, *enkai*, in the "Grayish-blue Stomach."

Religious symbols are multivocal, referring at the same time to more than one level of experience or order of knowledge, even referring to realities at opposite poles. "At one pole," writes Victor Turner, "referents are to social and moral facts, at the other, to physiological facts." The type of tree used in this fertility rite refers, among other things, obviously to breast milk with all its implications. Less patently it points to other realities suggesting generation, longevity, and the continuum of life through progenitors and progeny. Turner continues:

> Such symbols...unite the organic with the socio-moral order, proclaiming their ultimate religious unity, over and above conflicts between and within these orders. Powerful drives and emotions associated with human physiology, especially with the physiology of reproduction, are divested in the ritual process of their anti-social quality, and attached to components of the normative order, energizing the latter with a borrowed vitality....Symbols are both the resultants and the instigators of this process, and encapsulate its properties.[33]

The ritual generation of new fire, noted previously, as also the symbolism of wetness, may be seen in this light.

PROPHETS

In the face of the vast unknown enveloping so much of human experience, past, present and future, every sociocultural community finds ways to explain and to cope with the mystery of evil and the ominous signs encountered in the course of life. Even the perplexities and anxieties arising from the ordinary sufferings, pains and ambiguities met at every stage of the human sojourn need plausible explanations and remedies that are at least hopeful, if not always effective. In the absence of the religious beliefs, and the scientifically grounded laws, theories, and hypotheses used in the modern western world to explain the hidden factors influencing life and sometimes yielding malign fruits, or causing catastrophic consequences, the traditional Maasai people rely not only on their religious beliefs and practices, but also on the skills of prophets, diviners, medicine and ritual experts. These several social functions are usually, but not always or exclusively, combined in the office of the prophet, *oloiboni* (pl. *iloibonok*).

As a social institution, these functionaries serve their community in constructive ways. They meet some of the very same basic needs that are met in culturally diverse ways by priests, scientists, and healers (both physical and psychological) in modern western societies. Among the Maasai, as everywhere else in the world, there are some professional practitioners who are greedy, impostors, quacks and charlatans, using their positions for their own enrichment by exploiting the ignorance of those who consult them. In general, however, and for the most part, the *iloibonok* may be seen as a positive institution serving real human needs. Even when they curse, *adek*, or use charms, *intalengo*, containing deadly medicine *entasim e setan*, or when they project harm onto someone just by their thoughts, the aim is supposed to be the protection of their clients against harm from curses, evil eyes and sorcery.

It is commonly assumed that the immediate causes of almost all afflictions, disasters and threats to life are nefarious intentions (e.g., envy, jealousy, revenge) arising from the hearts of wastrels, *ilwushuush*, "who have developed into malevolent freaks."[34] Such characters cannot be readily recognized, however. To protect society from their mischief, the special skills and powers of the *iloibonok* are required. And everyone knows that, if such skills and powers are used without sufficient justification, they are apt to lash back upon the *iloibonok* themselves.[35]

According to one of the best known Maasai myths in its most common version, the divinity is the original source of the powers of the *iloibonok*.[36] The connection with *Enkai* is through Kidongoi, the legendary founder of the *Enkidongi* family, *enkishomi*, which now amounts to a sub-clan of the *Ilaiser* clan, *olgilata*. Kidongoi, as a boy already circumcised, or as a childlike man, of unknown origin and parentage, was first encountered by the Maasai in the Ngong Hills or somewhere near there. Through his prophetic vision into the unknown and a variety of miraculous or magical feats, he became in due course a revered patriarch. Also, or especially, he became a wise consultant and adviser to the Maasai people on problems and issues of all kinds.

Kidongoi's extraordinary gifts were handed on to selected sons whose own sons and grandsons continued to serve the people, generation after generation—as prophets (seers/clairvoyants), diviners, ritual experts, healers and advisers—having learned the profession from their fathers who enjoyed varying degrees of fame. The dominant *iloibonok* today are the descendants of Olonana (d. 1912) and Sendeu (d. 1937). These two famous historical figures were sons of Mbatiany (d. 1881)[37] who is said to have foretold the coming of white invaders and the hard times that started around the turn of the century. Because of their alleged link with the divinity, and the reports of their historical accomplishments, the whole *Enkidongi* family, particularly the practitioners of their inherited gifts and skills, still inspire a certain amount of awe and fear among most Maasai people, even among those in the modern sector developed under the influence of twentieth-century colonialism, missionary activity, schooling, and the current cash economy. Accordingly, the varied services of *iloibonok* are still called upon by all sections, clans and age groups of the population. Their guidance is especially needed in relation to rites of passage and fertility rituals.

On the occasion of extraordinary calamities, however, another type of prophet, not of the *Enkidongi* family, has been known to emerge with even greater, but more temporary, religious influence than the *iloibonok*. At least two such prophets, reminiscent of the prophetic ministry recorded in the Old Testament, achieved prominence throughout Maasailand in Kenya and Tanzania during recent decades.[38] The convergence of large-scale tragedy with the naiveté of such prophets gives their messages a world-shaking potential not yet activated, because the prophets, up to now, have not been acutely aware of the political causes behind the socioeconomic plight of the entire Maasai people. The first of these prophets arose in the early 1960s after a severe drought which was followed by famines and floods. The second arose in 1990, as the people became more generally and explicitly, although not yet explosively, conscious of the progressive pauperization they were chronically suffering due to the relentless alienation of their traditional dry season grazing lands for the benefit of others.

Both of these men were preliterate traditionalists from undistinguished families. Moreover, and surprisingly in a gerontocracy, at the time of their emergence from obscurity, they both belonged to an age group of warriors, *ilmurran*. Their messages, admonitions and warnings addressed generally to the whole Maasai population were similar. Both also claimed divine sanctions, calling the people back to the authentic cultural traditions that had sustained them historically. While challenging neither the religious innovations introduced by Christian missionaries, nor the modern governing authorities, they called particularly for a return to the prayerful ways of their own original religious practices, customs, and mores.

At one time in the early 1960s, the whole Maasai people, section by section, location by location, went on retreat, praying intensively for several days according to the young prophet's prescribed prayer formulas and ritual actions. Even the schools had to be closed during these days, at least in

Tanzania's Maasai District, as all Maasai children were called home for the required prayer sessions, and for the ritual slaughtering of specially chosen sheep on the last of the prescribed days. The implications of the 1990 prophecies are not yet clear to outside observers, except that *Enkai* is regarded unquestionably as their Originator.

Enkai communicates with these prophets, as she does sometimes with *iloibonok*, in dreams. Again, we are reminded of important information and warnings communicated, according to the Bible, in the same way. See, for example, Matthew's gospel (2:7, 12–13, 19, 22). Another method employed exclusively by *iloibonk* for gaining access to knowledge not normally available to ordinary mortals is by reading the configurations of small piles of tiny stones shaken out from the special container, *enkidong*, used variously for divination. This has some resemblance to the popular western practice of trying, through astrology, to get hold of naturally hidden information, even not yet existing information about the future.

SOME CONCLUSIONS

The foregoing notes and reflections are merely summary indicators of what Maasai religious experience is all about. They suggest why and how indigenous African symbols and rituals are capable of withdrawing people from the "banalized ordinariness" of everyday life. Indeed, this is the role of religion, as a system of culturally rooted symbols and actions relating persons to the ultimate conditions of their existence.[39] It is a creative effort of humankind's analogical imagination to open new vistas to the authentic meaning of life, and to propound the holy mystery of humankind's transcendent aspirations.

Maasai religion seeks to do this by revealing a path to the "Really Real" which is reached through paradigmatic rituals grounded and symbolized in such mundane realities as north, south, east, west, sky, clouds, stars, moon, sun, rain, earth, grass, trees, shells, animals, fire, smoke, blood, bones, beads, hides, water, milk, honey, meat, mead, people; also through the memory of the originating events of the human sojourn.[40] Such a culturally integrated and ecologically sensitive symbol system provides its people with a plausible wisdom tradition; it "grounds them in values that transcend the immediate needs and purposes of society," enabling them to hold out against alien forces bearing superficial and disconcerting messages.[41] At the same time, adequate space is allowed for the integration of culturally and religiously compatible innovations, modifications, additions and constructions. The next chapter offers suggestions on the real possibility of reconceptualizations and reinterpretations aimed at the genuine incarnation of Christianity in Maasai cultural terms.

IV

Possible Applications

To use simply the resources of one's own culture is not to communicate with the other....Nor is it enough simply to employ the
resources of the other culture. One must do so creatively.

—Bernard Lonergan [1]

In the present post-colonial climate it should be possible to rethink critically the history of the expansion of Christianity among the peoples of the
south. It should even be possible now to present the good news of Jesus
Christ "creatively" to a people: to express it and celebrate it among them,
without at the same time asking them "to renounce their own culture" with
its immemorial "religious riches." This is precisely what "one must do" as a
missionary or pastor serving today in a non-western cultural zone. God's
love for humankind, as manifest in the incarnational mission of the divine
Word, allows people to be themselves in their particular historical and cultural situations. And people need to be themselves, if they are to retain their
psychosocial balance in the face of life's varied sounds and furies. So, the
only thing to be renounced by new Christians is sinful behavior, or any cultural element found to be clearly and demonstrably "contrary to the Gospel."[2]

It is not enough to present Christianity to a people in their own language, understood in a merely semantic or literary sense. A more comprehensive language—in the "anthropological sense" employed by Pope Paul
VI—must also be appreciated, assumed and used. This language consists of
the people's indigenous cultural symbols, signs, myths, rites, images, customs and gestures. Also included here are the "aspirations, riches, limita-

tions, ways of praying, loving, looking at life and the world which distinguish this or that human gathering." These are the appropriate means of religious communication with any people.[3]

Why are these things so important? Because any society's coherence and continuity depend upon the loyalty of its members to their own indigenous symbol systems, especially in the realm of religion, even when these cultural inventions suffer from "gaps, insufficiencies and errors."[4] Intelligible and affective communication is compromised to the extent that the people lose respect for their own traditional meaning systems. Without such communication, their common enterprise and view of reality are gradually and irretrievably lost. Inevitably, then, their community disintegrates. This point is spelled out concisely by Avery Dulles in these few illuminating sentences:

> The psychology of images is exceedingly subtle and complex. In the religious sphere, images function as symbols....They speak to man existentially and find an echo in the inarticulate depths of his psyche. Such images communicate through their evocative power. They convey a latent meaning that is apprehended in a non-conceptual, even a subliminal, way. Symbols transform the horizons of man's life, integrate his perception of reality, alter his scale of values, reorient his loyalties, attachments and aspirations in a manner far exceeding the powers of abstract conceptual thought.[5]

If they are going to touch people profoundly, the imagery and symbolism used for communication and celebration "must be deeply rooted in the corporate experience of the faithful." They must resonate with the real human and religious experience of the people. But this can hardly happen when the symbol system is borrowed from the historically and culturally conditioned experience of some other people, ancient or modern. However, "if they do resonate," Dulles sees this as "proof that there is some isomorphism between what the image depicts and the spiritual reality with which the faithful are in existential contact."[6] This is dramatically demonstrated by the contrast between Africans singing conventional western hymns in church and the same people singing in their traditional styles during their customary rites of passage. A liturgy unrelated immediately to the culture of the celebrating community is apt to become what George B. Wilson calls "a totemized ritual—a lifeless shell fashioned out of somebody else's theology and priorities and aesthetic preferences, laid over the life of this community in a way that all but smothers its inner movements of the spirit."[7]

"Rituals there must be," says Bernard Cooke, if we are to celebrate the divine presence and communicate what this means to us as a people. "Ritual is intrinsic" to our human existence, because we are "symbol-making beings." Our religious rites are supposed to convey the meanings and to create the affective moods needed for awakening our sense of the divine presence, and for raising this sense to higher levels of consciousness and more lively intent. But all human creativity is constrained by the limited cultural resources and creative genius available to each people within their particular times and places. There is no such thing as a universally normative culture, one complex of symbol systems superior to all others. Nor is there—because all these things are historically conditioned cultural inventions—a single set of religious rites to which all peoples must conform in order to close the distance between God and humankind. That gap, according to the central belief of Christians, has already been closed. What remains is to celebrate and communicate this belief, thereby increasing our awareness of the divine proximity, the divinity-in-humanity. But this can be done only insofar as our culturally devised ritual signs are rooted in the everyday life and times of the celebrating community, and only insofar as the ritual celebrations relate to the people's "experienced sacredness of each day." This closing of the distance between God and ourselves is hardly accomplished by placing between us an alien system of symbolic communication.[8] How are people supposed to answer "amen" to blessings pronounced in a foreign tongue (I Cor 14:16)?

Of course, any people's traditional images and symbol systems are always subject to the relentless process of historical change. So a certain amount of ongoing research, reflection and updating is periodically necessary, if deep level communications are to be maintained by the church with its faithful communities where they are existentially. In the view of Father Dulles, the contemporary crisis of Christian faith experienced widely in the countries of the north is "in very large part a crisis of images."[9] The biblical imagery of lambs, wolves, shepherds, vines, grapes, kings and patriarchs hardly resonate deeply with the experience of the twentieth-century city dwellers of the world. Much less are these people in modern democratic societies comfortable with the archaic symbols and patriarchal styles of governance carried over from the medieval courts of European kings and princes.

Even more serious is the inability of many to resonate with the ancient but still dominant imagery used to explain, under the heading of redemption, the meaning of the life and death of Jesus. How often, widely and uncritically is this metaphor (buying back) used today as a simple explanation for the suffering and death of Jesus? The symbolic explanation of the transcendent reality of salvation in terms of God paying ransom to the devil with the blood of the Lamb was not, in the view of St. Anselm of Canterbury, satisfactory to the eleventh-century mentality of European Christians. Instead, Anselm's analogical imagination yielded new imagery borrowed from his own circumscribed time and place. This explanation has proven durable, but anyone who thinks about it is bound to wonder at the idea of our loving Father requiring the suffering and death of his beloved Son as the "price" to be paid as satisfaction for humankind's sins seen as affronts to the honor of God. Anselm's legalistic theory of satisfaction for the offended honor of a potentate is a good example of historically conditioned and culturally circumscribed theology; it presupposes the universal relevance of a "circle of ideas characteristic of feudalism."[10] Moreover, it is fraught with political implications that would certainly seem morally dubious to people in many other cultural worlds and historical periods.

According to Avery Dulles, "the notion of making reparation to the offended honor of God by offering up the blood of an innocent victim is more medieval than biblical." The meaning of redemption by the blood of Jesus in the New Testament is far more complex; it is embedded in the thought structures and communication patterns of a distant cultural world; it is "laden with connotations from the Exodus, the Temple worship and the Mosaic Law."[11] To discern the meaning is a daunting hermeneutical task which has in the course of history yielded a variety of metaphorical explanations. The discernment and appropriation of symbolized meanings is not just a matter of trusting in "eternally valid propositions" constructed in the past by western theologians. Instead, with Bernard Lonergan, we must place our trust "in the quite open structure of the human spirit"[12]—in a world saturated with grace. The central beliefs of the Christian tradition have to be thought out and articulated again in the historically conditioned and culture–specific terms of each people. Only then, when it is enfleshed in their own symbol systems, can people appropriate the authentic tradition, and hand it on to others.

If it is to be communicated to all peoples in their respective historical periods and cultural contexts, the meaning of what God has done in Jesus must be creatively reinterpreted and articulated through locally intelligible symbols already operative in the existing culture of each people, and this must be done also for successive generations. Of course, there will be differences of interpretation and articulation, as there have always been down through the ages, as also in the New Testament itself. Such culture-specific and historically conditioned differences, strange concepts and local idiosyncrasies, far from threatening the unity of faith, "rather...testify to its vitality," says Bernard Lonergan: "Doctrines that really are assimilated bear the stamp of those that assimilate them, and the absence of such an imprint would point to a merely perfunctory assimilation." This is so because "human concepts and human courses of action are products and expressions of acts of understanding; human understanding develops over time; such development is cumulative, and each cumulative development responds to the human and environmental conditions of its place and time."[13]

Again, this is not to say that everything in each culture is to be assumed uncritically and integrated somehow into the life of the church. Every society, including those of Europe and North America, has elements that are evidently *contrary* to the teachings of Jesus. While asking people to recognize their sins and repent, missionaries and pastors must themselves learn to recognize and renounce their too tolerant attitudes toward the *contrary* elements in their own societies and in their own personal lives. They must also learn to see and repent their own lack of cultural sensitivity. This is difficult when ethnocentrism, which is a congenital human affliction, has hardened into cultural arrogance producing delusions of human superiority. Even this can be overcome, however, if there is a will to look self-critically at what we have been doing in the name of Christ to African cultures for more or less one hundred years.

There is reason for hope. Full-time engagement in cross- cultural ministries these days can awaken missionaries and pastors to a positive appreciation of the cultural worlds of the peoples to whom they have been sent. Otherwise, they tend to return home rather soon, or to distract themselves with irrelevant hobbies. Among those remaining in the field, and retaining a willingness to learn from the people, some will eventually come to appreciate not only the rationality but also the signs of God's activity in culturally diverse ways of being human and religious. Thus, for example, instead of simply condemning, as "witchcraft" or "black magic," the activities of local healers and prophets, they will learn to consider these social institutions from the vantage point of the people. In many cases, then, they will find that African healers and prophets are performing for their people the same functions provided by psychiatrists and psychological counselors in the countries of the north. Instead of dismissing as "heathenism" the traditional social and religious rites of the people, they will come to see these celebrations as symbolic structures of social cohesion, as ways of affirming faith in God, and as defenses against anomie. They might also learn that amulets and bodily markings function, for many Africans, in much the same way that the carrying of religious medals, rosary beads and rabbit feet function for many Europeans and North Americans. These are devices for warding off evil and promoting good luck; they are psycho-social and culturally approved ways of generating a measure of emotional security in a world full of threats.

BORROWING AND CHANGING

To affirm the priority of each people's local symbol systems is not to deny the importance of elements borrowed from other cultures, and the innovations thereby introduced. "Priority" should not be interpreted as exclusiveness. Nor are innovations something to be avoided. Both borrowing and changing, probably more often than not, contribute to the vitality of any society. Instead of trying always to avoid them, innovations may be seen generally as things to be integrated in the life of society. The message of Jesus, however understood or misunderstood, has been a great force for change historically. This has been so even when Christianity was presented by means and methods subversive of its own mission and damaging to the people it intended "to save."

According to Robert J. Schreiter, "the imagery of Christian eschatology, angelology, and demonology" is due to "the Persian influences upon Judaism." Indeed, like other religions, "Christianity...has a long history of absorbing elements (syncretism) from the cultures in which it has lived." Against this historical background, the insistent questions concerning the ongoing inculturation or contextualization of Christianity in the cultural world of the south are forthrightly asked by Professor Schreiter in his challenging book, *Constructing Local Theologies*:

> Is our problem now that the same process (pluralistic borrowing and constant changing) is continuing, but that things are happening too quickly and many more cultures are involved? A related question has to be asked: Who determines what is proper and improper borrowing?[14]

However they eventually deal with it, many people find change hard to accept, perhaps because every change foreshadows our mortality. Reminders of human finitude can be disconcerting. This thought is a source of anxiety worldwide: that whatever has a beginning in time also terminates in time. Accordingly, all sorts of reasons for inhibiting change are apt to be conjured up. Against the kinds of changes proposed in this book, some missionaries and pastors are bound to object that their people like things the way they are. This defense of the *status quo* was heard frequently in the face of the innovations mandated by the Second Vatican Council. One may also recall the anxiety caused in the late 1940s by the movement for the introduction of vernacular languages in place of the Latin of the Roman Catholic liturgy. Even in Africa, during the following decades, the change from Gregorian chant in Latin to modern church music was a slow process. Still, there is much hesitation before the next logical step: the introduction of purely African styles of song and dance. Although much of the resistance is tacit, the perennial Euro-American ethnocentrism occasionally shows itself in a standard objection against all innovations. It is asserted simplistically that such radical changes, as are proposed in this book, would lead the people back into the darkness of "paganism" from which they had so recently been rescued by imitating western ways of being religious.

COURAGE REQUIRED

Some of the questions raised by the incarnational approach are obviously more difficult, emotionally as well as theologically and historically, than others in our invincibly pluralistic world. Is it really a matter of God's will for the Arctic Inuit and for desert nomads in Africa to celebrate the eucharist with grape wine and wheat bread, for example; or for Christians everywhere to conceptualize and structure their marriages according to a strictly western (basically pre-Christian Mediterranean) sociocultural model of the man-woman relationship?[15] Where polygyny is customary, would it not be possible, asks Karl Rahner, "for an African chief, even if he is a Christian, to live in the style of the Patriarch Abraham?" In another rhetorical question, Rahner points to one of the major pastoral issues facing the church today in all parts of Africa: "Must the marital morality of the Maasai of East Africa be substantially no more than a repetition of the morality of European Christianity...?"[16] In Rahner's essay, as in this book, the Maasai stand symbolically for many other peoples.

As already indicated in previous chapters, there are many other areas in which, with much less controversy, it should be possible to make room for non-western ways in the life of the church, or to initiate a genuine incarnation of Christianity in the real lives of African peoples. Dialogue and collaboration with the followers of traditional religions, as mandated by Vatican II, would surely be an obvious starting point.[17]

The courage needed for all such initiatives will be found in a proper theological understanding of the nature of the church as a continuation (in sacramental symbolism) of the incarnational mission of the divine Word who, according to Christian revelation, wills to speak to humanity in the real physical and cultural flesh of each tribe and tongue and people and nation. This outward-looking ecclesiology presupposes not only the sociological validity and psychological necessity of traditional African cultures, with their pluriform social structures and religious symbols, but also presupposes the efficacious operations of divine grace in and through the history of these cultures. It is, after all, an enormous conceit to imagine that western cultural ways were more appropriate for God's self-communication than are the ways of humankind's vast majority.

Courage in this context may be identified practically with the hope that drives and sustains faith, which is never without some risk. In the words of Karl Rahner, "courage, understood in its existential necessity and radical nature, is in fact what is called faith in Christian theology."[18] Christians, including pastors, missionaries, theologians and high level office holders in the church, are expected to live according to faith, with all the risks entailed, even when no one is applauding their efforts, and even when they are suffering persecution.

ALSO RESEARCH

More than courage is needed, of course. Much careful research is required, too, as well as serious reflection and open discussion. It is presumptuous and magical to believe that the Holy Spirit guides us when we do not use our normal human faculties, gifts and skills in pursuing truth and discerning God's will. Far from undermining the faith and practice of the church, the very difficulties raised by the principle of incarnation can, as the fathers of Vatican II learned and taught, "stimulate the mind to a more accurate and penetrating grasp of the faith." So it is both appropriate and necessary to make use "not only of theological principles, but also of the findings of the secular sciences."[19] Because of the methods and findings of the modern social sciences, particularly in the areas of anthropology, sociology, psychology and history, our intellectual horizons today are apt to be far wider than those of our predecessors, so many of whom were socialized into and trapped within the "classicist" worldview.

This is why the council directed that new theological commissions be set up, and new studies initiated, "in each major socio-cultural area," bringing to bear "a fresh scrutiny" on the deeds and words of sacred scripture, the church fathers and the teaching authority of the church. Faith seeking understanding through such an intercultural reexamination, aided by the philosophies, traditions, wisdom, experiences, customs and worldviews of non-western peoples, will open new avenues "for a more profound adaptation in the whole area of Christian living."[20]

Mistakes will be made. But these will not be worse than the old mistake of ignoring the incarnational nature of the Christian world mission, while simplistically urging people to imitate western cultural patterns and ethnic conventions. If the initial efforts at incarnating the faith in the local cultures are tentatively worked out with the people themselves, and recognized by all as tentative, then any mistakes can be corrected in the way that the translations of biblical texts into African languages are regularly corrected without any paralyzing fears of syncretism or heterodoxy.

There is much evidence to suggest that history will continue to be made and shaped, as it always has been, by the decisions and actions of free and responsible agents responding boldly or timidly, out of courage or out of fear, with vision or in blindness, to the situations in which they find themselves, and according to the limited lights available during their brief moments in history. So it is with missionaries, pastors and various other Christian leaders in Africa today. They really do have the freedom to choose one approach or the other. They may continue transplanting the western experience of Christianity with the aim of turning African Christians into carbon copies of that experience. Or they may follow the more difficult and perhaps crucifying way of incarnation.

Theologically, it is all a matter of how one regards the principle of incarnation; whether or not this is seen as the central theme structuring the church. This, in turn, goes back to whether or to what extent one's faith and hope are rooted uniquely in the mystery of the incarnation. As Cardinal Otunga expressed it: "The basis for the incarnation of the Christian message into our African cultures is our Faith in the Incarnate Son of God."[21] The issue may also be put more concretely: either the church recognizes her need for the non-western cultures through which she is to become a World Church, and "accepts with a Pauline boldness the necessary consequences from this recognition, or it remains a Western Church and so in the last resort betrays the meaning of Vatican II."[22]

A EUROPEAN RELIGION OR A WORLD CHURCH?

Just as the New Testament records some inadequacies in the practice of the Jewish religion in the time of Jesus, and some basic misunderstandings among his first followers, so also theologians, and especially canon lawyers, are apt to find some "gaps, insufficiencies and errors" in the religious practices and perceptions of the Maasai. But the few Catholic missionaries working among these people are inclined to view the people's religious system as basically compatible with the central beliefs of Christianity.

Of course, as everywhere else in the world, there are recurring questions relating to the man-woman relationship. As in the countries of the north, so also in Africa, Christians are chronically faced with morally or religiously questionable extramarital sexual practices. Everywhere also there are unfair social structures and unjust patterns of behavior arising from sins of avarice, envy, calumny and detraction. In many places the conceptualization and structuring of marriage raises major questions. In much of Africa, marriage is a prolonged process. Among some peoples, as with the ancient Jews, the marriage process is consummated only with the birth of a male child. Plural marriage (polygamy) is another problematical practice found throughout the world. Among most of Africa's peoples, this takes the form of simultaneous polygyny (more than one wife at the same time). Among Europeans and Americans plural marriage takes the form of consecutive polygyny and consecutive polyandry (one spouse after another).

In the face of all such behavior, as we know from the history of Christianity in the west, a great measure of patience and even tolerance is possible. We may recall, for example, that the buying and selling of kidnapped human beings was not always considered sinful by Christians. The Catholic bishops of the United States, on the eve of the war between the States, "justified" slavery in a formal letter to the U. S. Secretary of State. Even as late as 1866, the Vatican's Holy Office of the Sacred Inquisition was still confidently teaching the compatibility of slavery with Christianity.[23] The transformation of social consciousness is a gradual process. The fruits of evangelization are supposed to occur in each cultural world in a manner analogous to the action of a leaven gradually transforming the mass of dough from within. Bread cannot be produced by either ignoring or rejecting the ingredients that give a loaf its shape, texture, color, taste and durability. The time needed for this transformation must also be respected. Neither can evangelization be achieved, much less the building of a World Church, by either ignoring or rejecting the actually existing cultural worlds of humankind's vast majority living outside the walls of ancient Christendom.

So the question here is not whether or to what extent the religious experience and moral behavior of African peoples, either before or after the advent of Christian missionaries among them, is perfectly in accord with some religious and ethical ideals conceptualized by European theologians and labeled "Christian." The question concerns the extent to which

Christianity can be understood, lived, expressed and celebrated by African peoples in their own indigenous ways of being human and religious, without having to rely massively and perpetually upon imported cultural baggage from Europe and North America. In broad terms, the question is whether or to what extent the Christian churches, historically rooted in western cultural worlds, are willing to become in historical tangibility a genuine World Church, authentically universal and truly catholic in cultural terms.

WHICH MEMORIAL RITE OF THANKSGIVING AND COMMUNION?

To suggest what the Christian liturgy might look like, were it really enfleshed in one of Africa's many different cultural worlds today, we might consider, for example, how the ritual slaughtering of animals, as traditional and religiously significant events among the Maasai, could be assumed, "baptized," and officially recognized as the eucharistic celebration of Maasai Christians. In its primary meaning, the eucharist is a memorial meal celebrating the Christian community's gratitude for their new life of hope in unity with the risen Lord. With reference to the historical example provided by Jesus at the last supper, a Christian transformation of the religious symbol system described in the previous chapter of this volume should be possible. Such a transformation might even be required by the principle of inculturation—in obedience to the incarnational mission entrusted by Christ to the church. While retaining the traditional structure of the Maasai rite, the content of meaning could be transformed into an indigenous experience of Christian faith. Analogously this is what happens whenever the good news of Jesus is presented in the terms of another language. The linguistic system of communication remains what it has always been, but it conveys entirely new meanings to the believing community.

Appropriate modification of meaning could be made, for example, by reformulating the content of some typical Maasai prayers, with a view to emphasizing the appropriate Christian themes and the important moments of the sacramental enactment: *anamnesis, epiclesis, koinonia* and the "great amen." No need for such culture-specific accoutrements as imported food, drink, linen, table, chairs, candles, chalice, ciborium, cruets and vestments. If pre-Christian styles of dress, modeled on the garb of ancient Greco-Roman authority figures, are suitable for the Christian liturgy even today in the north, then the traditional religious garb of various African peoples might also be considered seemly in Africa. The ancient Mediterranean peoples felt that white and various bright colors were religiously significant, but the Maasai favor black or dark blue. Fur copes made of hyrax skins are often worn by Maasai celebrants on solemn ritual occasions. Of course, a copy of the Bible in the local language would be significant. As the whole Bible is not yet available in the Maasai language, the parts already translated, particularly of the New Testament, should suffice for the liturgy of the word. But consideration could be given to the feasibility of incorporating into this liturgy some references to Maasai history and traditional mythology. Otherwise, everything needed for a meal of meaningful celebration is readily available from the religious traditions of the Maasai.

The traditional ritual slaughtering of animals on major ceremonial occasions is certainly a religious rite, symbolically enacting what is signified. God's presence and generosity to the people is at the center of attention. The flesh and blood from their domestic animals here and now actually continue to sustain the people's lives in a shared meal recalling God's original gift of domestic livestock which, in the subsistence economy of these people, signify the gift of life. These activities probably contain, and reflect in their own historico-cultural way, the same basic meanings intended in the Thanksgiving Day rites of North Americans. Not only the particular items eaten for both sustenance and enjoyment, but also the praying, singing and dancing point to the common beginnings of the people, and to their hopeful future. This shared memorial meal recalls and celebrates how the life of the people has been, on account of God's goodness, from the beginning of their historical sojourn, and also how it should be now and in the days ahead. The available evidence certainly does not warrant the assumption that this rite is the same as the sin offerings of the ancient Jews. The ritual slaughtering by the Maasai need not be interpreted as a way of making propitiatory "deals" with God. The victim and its consumption evidently symbolize the communion of the people with God, and their thanksgiving for divine blessings. The slaughtered animal serves as a pledge of the people's total surrender to God. If this is true worship, culturally created but also graced, then it is capable of being assumed, assimilated and transformed by faith in Jesus Christ.

As with all ritual enactments, it may appear that many people, while correctly performing the actions, miss the meanings. This may be so on the level of conceptual intelligibility and explicit consciousness. But symbolic communication, operating with multiple signals on the level of immediate experience, reaffirms the celebrants' sense of corporate solidarity and common destiny before God and the rest of humankind. Although ardent feelings of group solidarity may be more evident in Maasai rites, an intensified awareness of the divine presence is the important religious effect of these ritual enactments. A people's consciousness of this presence is what Bernard Cooke calls "the core of the symbolizing religious experience." Whether Christian or not, worship is essentially a matter of acknowledging and honoring God by manifesting openness to the divine presence as signaled in culturally invented and historically conditioned symbol systems.[24]

The traditional Maasai rite of thanksgiving should therefore be capable of reinterpretation, reconceptualization and transformation in a manner analogous to the way the early Mediterranean Christians transformed pre-Christian ideas and symbols, such as covenant, *logos*, sacrifice and baptism. They did this by building upon, not destroying, the earlier meanings of these terms, even as the ancient Hebrews had done with elements from the religious experience of the Canaanites.[25] This type of transformation in the realm of ritual is exemplified by the new meaning given gradually by Christians to the Jewish Passover meal. Even in the time of St. Paul, this process of transformation was already operating. Without forgetting the original Jewish meaning of the paschal feast, a new meaning is added by the community of Christian believers. For them, the old Passover meal becomes also the new paschal feast: the "Supper of the Lord" (cf. I Cor 5:8; 10:16; 11:20). The essential structure remains with its traditional layers of meaning, but it now has the additional significance of a memorial meal of thanksgiving for the life, death and resurrection of the Lord in union with the community of his witnesses.[26] There is some analogy here with the transformation occurring when a non-Christian person is evangelized and baptized. The person remains essentially the same, but now she or he has a transformed consciousness and self-understanding guided by new meanings and expectations in life.

Through experimental liturgies, traditional gestures and decorations, as well as selected styles of dancing and singing, would easily enough find their appropriate places in such a renewed ritual performance. This does not mean that Christianity's previous layers of symbolic meaning, inherited from Jewish and other Mediterranean traditions, should be ignored; only that the Maasai symbol system should be, for the Maasai, the top layer. So it should be, because rituals that really speak to the heart are rooted in, and emerge from historically conditioned human experience in the familiar cultural worlds of particular peoples. Alien rituals cannot speak to a people as profoundly as their own traditional ways of approaching the ultimate sources of meaning in their lives.[27] The idea of Maasai Christians retaining their pre-Christian rites and practices is not unthinkable when seen in the light of the church's early history. Even the Christian understanding of sacrifice "has remained fraught with the ambiguities of a checkered history," as we learn from Robert J. Daly:

As the centuries passed many of the institutional, cultic phenom-
ena associated with the Old Testament and even pagan priest-
hood and sacrifice found their way into Christian practice.[28]

The foregoing paragraphs touch upon some of the principal theoretical
points to be considered regarding the feasibility of applying the principle of
inculturation to the religious situation of people in the real world. What is the
meaning of the church's incarnational mission among the nations, if it does
not entail the assumption and transformation of the particular non-Christian,
or pre-Christian, symbol systems? The model used for demonstrating the
urgency of this question is the previous historical assumption and transformation of Jewish and Greco-Roman religious forms and structures in the
course of Christianity's historical expansion in the north. Surely the same
incarnational process is valid among the far more numerous peoples in the
south.

SOME FINAL CONSIDERATIONS

There are also some practical points to think about. It might be found,
for example, that once a week would be too often for such a rich liturgy to be
repeated. Besides, the Maasai do not live in large population clusters. As
semi-nomads they are spread out over large grazing ranges (well over 10,000
square miles in Kenya, and much more than that in Tanzania). Their major
ceremonial events require considerable preparation and expense, as people
living at some distance must be accommodated at least for a couple of days.
Maasai ritual enactments are also social gatherings involving much more
than forty minutes once a week.

Maasai time is measured by moons, not weeks, and also by historical
events and relational experiences—not by the rigid nothings of clocks and
calendars.[29] "If the experience of time is perceived differently by various cultures," notes John M. Huels, "it seems likely that canon law might well be
interpreted differently by people who do not share its view of time."[30]
Accordingly, it might be found that the central liturgical celebration of
Maasai Christians could most suitably be held only two or three times a year
in each of the suitable places chosen by the people for this purpose. No need
for great buildings. A few shade trees would suffice, as they do now for traditional Maasai ceremonies which are certainly more alive with meaning
than the bookish rites imported from Europe and still used slavishly inside
most mission compounds and parish churches.

Of course, the details of such a proposal would have to be discussed at length with the local people most in touch with their own traditions. Even theological debates might be appropriate for surfacing problems, clarifying issues and answering questions. Considerable research might thus be called for. There is also a need for more patience with, and respect for, the church leaders and theologians currently wrestling with the new questions posed by the social sciences. The relevant literature, for example, would have to be reviewed on such questions as the appropriate elements to be used in an authentically African eucharistic rite.[31] Should it be the food and drink of the ancient Passover meal of the Jews, or should it be, for a particular African people, the religiously significant food and drink used traditionally in their own indigenous rite of thanksgiving?

Moreover, the extent to which the ritual slaughtering of animals by the Maasai should or should not be construed as "sacrificial" in any sense incompatible with Christianity would need further inquiry.[32] In this regard it would also have to be decided which of the diverse meanings of the word "sacrifice" is normative for such an inquiry.[33] Modern scholars know that this is a formidable task, as rituals labelled "sacrifice" are virtually universal, so the word has countless denotations and connotations: cultic, spiritual, secular, poetic. "In different places and periods," writes Edward Hulmes, "the word refers to human activities directed to different ends, and proceeding from different motives."[34] These varied meanings are so self-evident to insiders that they hardly bother to conceptualize them in abstract philosophical terms. Foreigners, who are not personal participants in the religious rites of a particular community, especially if they already have their own cultural definition of sacrifice, are apt to miss the meanings, as they try to fit them into alien categories of thought.

Another question is whether "spiritualized" sacrifice alone (inside the human psyche) suffices for Christians everywhere; or to what extent animal sacrifice, where this is a cultural tradition, might also be appropriate—as it might well have been among the Jewish Christians of Jerusalem, at least until the destruction of the Temple in A.D. 70 (cf. Acts 2:46; 3:1–4; 21:24–26: 22:17). It is noteworthy that Jesus, after curing a man's skin disease, had no hesitation in sending him to the Temple to make the customary animal sacrifices prescribed by Moses (Mt 8:4; Mk 1:34; Lev 14:1–23). In any case, since meat offered to idols may be eaten by Christians, *a fortiori* it is permissible for them to eat meat offered to God, especially where this is the appropriate food for festive occasions. This whole question of the compatibility of Christianity with the traditional religious practices of the Maasai,[35] and of so many other African peoples, should be seen in the light of the pre-Christian practices of the first followers of Jesus, as noted by Hans Küng:

> They (the first Christians) *were* already the new Israel, even if externally little different from the old. In the light of this saving event which had already occurred they could remain members of the people of Israel, share in its cult, keep its laws, affirm its history and its expectations—and yet see all those things in a fundamentally new way because of Jesus Christ. They could retain the Jewish forms and yet give them an entirely new content...."[36]

The role of the venerable elders as religious leaders of Maasai society, a gerontocracy, would also have to be considered in light of the New Testament requirements for positions of leadership in Christian communities (1 Tim 3:12; Titus 1:6). These pastoral norms contrast sharply with the present system determined by church law. What is done now in this gerontocracy—in keeping with the church's universal canonical requirements—is to impose upon the Christian community religious leaders belonging to the most junior age groups: men resocialized by their schooling and seminary experiences, ill-informed about the customs and traditions of their own people, although very knowledgeable in the ways of the west. Nor have these young and unmarried Maasai priests been tested against the local norms of maturity and responsibility in an inhospitable environment, with a vulnerable subsistence economy, and a precarious political future.

In the light of what was said in chapter three concerning the socio-religious role of Maasai elders in their society, George Wilson's comments on religious leadership are germane here:

> The power to lead is *conferred* by any people on those who deeply respect the heritage, genius and ethos of those they are called to lead. It is *earned* through sensitivity, reverent listening and regard for the otherness of the community, not claimed on the basis of oils on one's hands or letters after one's name. The reality is that the spirit has been praying within this particular people, shaping them through their particular experiences, long before the prayer leader arrived....Leaders do not create prayer, they invoke it in people fashioned and claimed by God....The leader's role is to invite the people into the search, not to bring them a bag of trinkets to distract them from the God who is waiting to be found and acknowledged and celebrated.[37]

None of the foregoing suggestions need be construed as necessarily excluding most of the adaptations of the Roman rite currently in use. There are situations in which a culturally incarnated liturgy may not always be feasible—although such exceptions should not be treated as normative. For practical reasons arising from the circumstances of particular times and places, fully incarnated liturgies might have to be reserved for special occasions such as the feasts of the resurrection and Pentecost. There must be room for diversity and varied patterns of liturgical organization.

The imperialistic imposition of a uniform pattern on all peoples everywhere is no longer tolerable; it is bound to do more harm than good, as it contradicts the church's own need to be fully at home in the cultural world of each distinctive people. African cultures, as indeed all cultures, are constantly undergoing changes; so, also on the practical level, flexibility is required of ecclesial communities "always in need of reform."

Real unity in faith and belief is best safeguarded not by rigid uniformity of practices, but by respectful pluralism. It must also be clearly recognized that adaptation is no substitute for inculturation, if we are really serious about the implications of the incarnation of the divine Word, and about the church's call to authentic cultural catholicity.

Whatever the problems to be faced, the general idea of attempting something along these lines is surely what is meant by inculturation as a way of making the gospel incarnate in different cultures.[38] Indeed, the very point of this radical incarnation is the full acceptance of the people where they are, in their own time and place, in everything except sin. Such is the incarnational economy through which God embraces humankind from within. "From now on," according to John Paul II, "the Church opens her doors and becomes the house which all may enter, and in which all can feel at home, while keeping their own cultures and traditions, provided these are not *contrary* to the Gospel."[39]

Such a proposal, however shocking to the "classicist mentality," is much less astonishing and no more scandalous than the original physical, cultural and historical enfleshment of the divine Word, which is Christianity's primordial sacramental paradigm and model for all missionary and pastoral activity—indeed for every encounter between God and humankind. The incarnational way of reinterpreting, reconceptualizing and transforming the meanings of pre-Christian symbols, myths and rituals, discussed nowadays under the heading of inculturation, is not a modern invention; it is a discovery of what has been going on from the very beginning of the Christian movement, and before that in the history of Judaism. This is abundantly exemplified both in the Bible and in the history of the expansion of Christianity among the gentiles of the Mediterranean basin.[40] Even in that small segment of humankind, the early church was relatively more pluriform in its cultural incarnations than it is in the much larger world of our time. We are reminded of this by a famous passage from the *Letter to Diognetus* (c. A.D. 200):

> For Christians cannot be distinguished from the rest of the human race by country or language or customs. They do not live in cities of their own; they do not use a peculiar form of speech; they do not follow an eccentric form of life....Yet, although they live in Greek and barbarian cities alike, as each man's lot has been cast, and follow the customs of the country in clothing and food and other matters of daily living, at the same time they give proof of the remarkable and admittedly extraordinary constitution of their own commonwealth.[41]

Notes

INTRODUCTION

1. John Paul II, *Redemtor hominis* (Vatican City, March 4 1979), nos. 13–14.

2. Vatican Council II, "Decree on the Church's Missionary Activity," *Ad gentes* (Vatican City, December 7, 1965), no. 10.

3. *Ibid.*, no. 22.

4. International Theological Commission, "Faith and Inculturation," in *Origins,* vol. 18, no. 47 (May 4, 1989), pp. 800–807.

5. John Paul II, "Episcopal Ministry at the Service of Life," address in Nairobi to the Bishops of Kenya (7 May 1980) in *Africa: Apostolic Pilgrimage,* compiled speeches (Boston: Daughters of St. Paul, 1980) p. 243.

6. Karl Rahner, "Perspectives for Pastoral Theology in the Future," *Theological Investigations* 22, trans. Joseph Dunceel (New York: Crossroad, 1991), p. 109.

7. Walter Brueggemann, "A Gospel Language of Pain and Possibility," in *Horizons of Biblical Theology,* vol. 13, no. 2 (December 1991), p. 95.

8. Paul VI, apostolic exhortation *Evangelii nuntiandi* (Vatican City, December 8 1975) no. 20, as quoted by John Paul II, in his encyclical letter *Redemptoris missio* (Vatican City, December 7, 1990), no. 37c.

9. Bernard Lonergan, "Unity and Plurality: The Coherence of Christian Truth," in *A Third Collection,* edited by F. E. Crowe (New York: Paulist Press, 1985) p. 243. See also Paul VI, *Evangelii nuntiandi,* nos. 20, 63.

10. Lesslie Newbigin, "Can the West be Converted?" in *International Bulletin of Missionary Research ,* vol. 11, no. 1 (January 1987) pp. 2–7. On this issue, see also John A. Coleman, "Inculturation and Evangelization in the North American Context," in *Catholic Theological Society of America: Proceedings of the 45th Annual*

Convention (Louisville: CTSA, 1990), pp. 15–29; Gregory Baum, *Theology and Society* (New York: Paulist Press, 1987), pp. 195–205; and Gustavo Gutierrez, *The Truth Shall Make You Free,* trans. Matthew J. O'Connell (Maryknoll, New York: Orbis Books, 1990), pp. 110–116.

1. THE COLONIAL MODEL PERSISTING

1. Bernard Lonergan, *Method in Theology* (New York: Herder and Herder, 1972), pp. 362–363.

2. For details, see Thomas Pakenham, *The Scramble for Africa: 1876–1912* (New York: Random House, 1991), *passim.*

3. For some documented examples, see Richard D. Wolff, *The Economics of Colonialism: Britain and Kenya, 1870–1930* (New Haven: Yale University Press, 1974); W. McGregor Ross, *Kenya from Within: A Short Political History* (London: Frank Case, 1927, 1968); Norman Leys, *Kenya,* 4th edition (London: Frank Case, 1924); Richard W. Frank and Barbara H. Chasin, *Seeds of Famine: Ecological Destruction and the Development Dilemma in the West African Sahel* (Montclair, N.J.: Allenheld and Osmun, 1980); David Dalby and R.J. Harrison Church, eds., *Drought in Africa* (London: International African Institute, 1973).

4. Peter Berger and Thomas Luckmann, *The Social Construction of Reality: A Treatise on the Sociology of Knowledge* (New York and Harmondsworth: Penguin/Pelican. 1966–1984), p. 79.

5. *Ibid.* p. 80

6. Catholic Bishops of Zambia, Pastoral Letter, "'You Shall Be My Witnesses': A Second Century of Evangelization in Zambia," in *Catholic International,* vol. 2, No. 17 (October 1–14, 1991), p. 827, no. 20.

7. Eboussi Boulaga, *Christianity Without Fetishes: A Critique and Recapture of Christianity,* trans. Robert R. Barr (Maryknoll, N.Y.: Orbis Books, 1984), p. 17.

8. R. C. Wanjohi, *Evolution of Morals in Kenya Under the Influence of Christianity: A Developed Study of Agikuyu Morals and Marriages,* unpublished Ph.D. dissertation, Katholieke Universiteit Te Leuven, 1974, p. vii; see also pp. 83–88 on the Agikuyu name tradition.

9. Lawrence E. Sullivan, *Icanchu's Drum: An Orientation to Meaning in South American Religions* (New York: Macmillan Publishing Co.; London: Collier Macmillan, 1988), pp. 267, 638.

10. *Ibid.,* p. 638.

11. Joseph Ratzinger, "A Conversation with Joseph Ratzinger," in Teofilo Cabestrero, ed., *Conversations with Contemporary Theologians* (Maryknoll, New York: Orbis Books, 1981), p. 153. See also Yves Congar, *Christ, Our Lady and the Church: A Study in Eirenic Theology* (Westminster, Maryland: Newman Press, 1957), *passim*; Jerome Murphy-O'Conner, *Becoming Human Together* (Dublin: Veritas Publications, 1978), pp. 33–78; Karl Rahner, "The Position of Christology in

the Church between Exegesis and Dogmatics," *Theological Investigations,* 11 (London: Darton, Longman & Todd; New York: Seabury Press, 1974), pp. 194–199.

In his *Dynamics of Theology* (Paulist Press, 1990), Roger Haight attributes this monophysite tendency to the failure of most christologies to maintain the dialectical tension between the two natures in the person of Jesus. By resolving the tension in favor of the divinity, they abolish the God-in-humanity paradox, thus compromising Chalcedon's classical doctrine which is not an explanation of the status of Jesus. "It is rather," in Father Haight's words, "an assertion of the dimensions of Jesus' person and life that are purely dialectical...In so far as Jesus is a real human being, he is not God." Yet, he is "the normative embodiment of God in the world," making the divinity effectively present in his truly human being. "As in symbols generally, this dialectical tension cannot be resolved." Not without collapsing the symbol which Jesus is for humankind: God's loving presence among us, as one of us, in us and for us, in our global village with all of its historical and cultural implications (cf. pp. 139 & 258).

12.   Michael Schmaus, "Mariology," in Karl Rahner, Cornelius Ernst and Kevin Smyth, eds., *Sacramentum Mundi: An Encyclopedia of Theology* (New York and London: Herder and Herder, Burns and Oates, 1968), vol. III, p. 387. For more on the "erroneous developments and exaggerations" in the European forms of Marian devotions, see Heribert Muhlen, "New Directions in Mariology," *Theology Digest,* vol. 24, no. 3 (Fall 1976), pp. 286–292.

13.   Schmaus, *loc. cit.*

14.   My views on this are based on conversations with informed missionaries, and on the research of Peter J. Driven, *The Maria Legio: The Dynamics of a Breakaway Church among the Luo of East Africa,* unpublished doctoral dissertation (Rome: Pontificia Universitas Gregoriana, 1970), pp. 134, 226–227, 312–320. Driven notes in passing similar breakaway movements arising from, among other things, exaggerated devotions to the mother of Jesus: *Dini ya Shamuli* (Religion of the Flower), and a sect called Our Lady of Fatima.

15.   Congar, op. cit, pp. 60, 71.

16.   Lucien Deiss, *It's the Lord's Supper: Eucharist of Christians,* trans. Edmond Bonin (London: Collins Liturgical Publications, 1980), pp. 118, 104–130; Joseph A. Jungmann, *The Mass of the Roman Rite: Its Origins and Development,* trans. Francis A. Brunner and Charles K. Riepe, revised and abridged (New York: Benzinger Brothers, 1959), pp. 88–92, 107; and Tad W. Guzie, *Jesus and the Eucharist* (New York: Paulist Press, 1974), *passim.* See also Michael G. Lawler, *Symbol and Sacrament: A Contemporary Sacramental Theology* (New York: Paulist Press, 1987), pp. 33, 150.

17.   Karl Rahner, "On the Duration of the Presence of Christ after Communion," *Theological Investigations,* 4, p. 318. See also Lawler, *op. cit.,* p. 145: "Real presence is to be distinguished carefully from juxtaposition, being physically beside another person...."

18.   Avery Dulles, *Models of Revelation* (Garden City, New York: Doubleday, 1983), pp. 158–159.

19.   For the contemporary connotation of Pelagianism, see Thomas F. Schindler, *Ethics: The Social Dimension* (Wilmington, Delaware: Michael Glazier, 1989), p. 85;

and Thomas H. Groome, "Religious Education for Justice by Educating Justly," in Padraic O'Hare, *Education for Justice* (San Francisco: Harper and Row, 1983), p. 81. See also Karl Rahner and Herbert Vorgrimler, *Dictionary of Theology,* 2nd edition, trans. Richard Strachan, David Smith, Robert Nowell, and Sarah O'Brien Twohig (New York: Crossroad, 1981), p. 369: "Pelagianism is a sort of Stoic version of Pharisaism."

20. Karl Rahner, "Considerations on the Active Role of the Person in the Sacramental Event," *Theological Investigations,* 14 (London: Longman, Darton and Todd, 1976), pp. 182–183.

21. *Idem,* "Introductory Observations on Thomas Aquinas' Theology of the Sacraments in General," *Theological Investigations,* 14, p. 158.

22. *Idem,* "Considerations on the Active Role of the Person in the Sacramental Event," Theological Investigations, 14, pp. 179-180.

23. See Karl Rahner, "The Relationship Between Personal and Communal Spirituality in the Orders," *Theological Investigations* 14, pp. 222–223.

24. Gregory Baum, *Religion and Alienation: A Theological Reading of Sociology* (New York: Paulist Press, 1975), p. 196. On the "unjust structures," or the "structures of sin," resulting from this individualism, see John Paul II, encyclical letter *Laborem exercens* (1981), nos. 2, 7–8; encyclical letter *Sollicitudo rei socialis* (1987), nos. 11–40. See also Congregation for the Doctrine of the Faith, instruction *Libertatis conscientia* (1988), no. 13: "In the field of social and political achievements, one of the fundamental ambiguities of the affirmation of freedom in the age of the Enlightenment had to do with the concept of the subject of this freedom as an individual who is fully self-sufficient and whose finality is the satisfaction of its own interests in the enjoyment of earthly goods."

25. Aylward Shorter, *The African Synod: A Personal Response to the Outline Document* (Nairobi, St. Paul Publications—Africa, 1991), p. 58.

26. Baum, *Religion and Alienation,* p. 197. See Zachary Hayes, "Heaven," in Komonchak, *et al,* eds. *The New Dictionary of Theology* (Wilmington, Delaware: Michael Glazier, Inc., 1987) p. 456: "Heaven is not primarily a place but a personal relationship. The believer is 'in heaven' to the degree that he or she is with Christ; for it is in Christ that one finds an authentic relationship with God....The fulfillment symbolized by the word heaven does not mean the disappearance of the material world but its radical transformation." See also Joseph Ratzinger, *Eschatologie* (Regensburg, 1977), p. 190.

27. Vatican II, *Gaudium et spes,* "The Church in the Modern World," nos. 2, 40.

28. Karl Rahner, "Why and How Can We Venerate the Saints?" *Theological Investigations,* 8, trans. David Bourke (London: Longman, Darton and Todd; New York: Seabury, 1971), pp. 13–14.

29. *Idem, Nature and Grace* (London:Sheed and Ward, 1963), p.18.

30. Lonergan, *Method in Theology,* pp. 362–363.

31. As quoted in William J. Fulbright, *The Arrogance of Power* (New York: Random House, 1966), p. 18.

2. A RADICALLY NEW ATTITUDE

1. John Paul II, *Redemptoris missio,* encyclical letter on the mission of the Church (Vatican, December 7, 1990), no. 24.

2. *Ibid.,* nos. 25, 28.

3. Langdon Gilkey, *Through the Tempest: Theological Voyages in a Pluralistic Culture* (Minneapolis: Fortress Press, 1991), pp. 32, 181–182. See also World Council of Churches, *Guidelines on Dialogue with People of Living Faiths and Ideologies* (Geneva: WCC Publications, 1990). For recent reflections on Christian theology and African religious experience, see Lamin Sanneh, *Translating the Message: The Missionary Impact on Culture* (Maryknoll, New York: Orbis Books, 1989); Robert E. Hood, *Must God Remain Greek: Afro Cultures and God-Talk* (Minneapolis: Fortress Press, 1990); and Thomas C. Christensen, *An African Tree of Life* (Maryknoll, New York: Orbis Books, 1990).

4. On the creative use of the translation model, see Lamin Sanneh, *Translating the Message,* pp. 3, 71–81. For a more critical view of the method of Saints Cyril and Methodius, see Aylward Shorter, *Toward a Theology of Inculturation* (Maryknoll, New York: Orbis Books, 1988), pp. 143–145, 231–233.

5. Walter Brueggemann, "A Gospel Language of Pain and Possibility," in *Horizons in Biblical Theology,* vol.13, no. 2 (December 1991), p. 95. For more on the relationship between Christianity and culture, see H. Richard Niebuhr, *Christ and Culture* (New York: Harper and Row, 1951, 1956); and Paul Tillich, *Theology of Culture* (New York: Oxford University Press, 1964).

6. See Yves Congar, *The Mystery of the Temple: The Manner of God's Presence to His Creatures from Genesis to the Apocalypse,* trans. Reginald F. Trevett (London and Westminster, Md.: Newman Press, Burns and Oates, 1962), p. 299, n.7.

7. John Paul II, *Redemptoris missio,* nos. 28, 29.

8. Karl Rahner, "On the Theology of the Incarnation," *Theological Investigations,* 4 , trans. Kevin Smyth (London: Darton, Longman and Todd; New York: Seabury, 1974), p.105.

9. For a concise exposition of this principle, see Eugene Hillman, "Inculturation," in Joseph A. Komonchak, Mary Collins and Dermot A. Lane, eds., *The New Dictionary of Theology* (Collegeville: M. Glazier and Liturgical Press, 1987, 1991), pp. 510–513; International Theological Commission, "Faith and Inculturation," *Origins,* vol. 18, no. 47 (May 4, 1989), pp. 800–807. For a comprehensive treatment, see Aylward Shorter, *Toward a Theology of Inculturation;* Peter Schineller, *A Handbook on Inculturation* (New York: Paulist Press, 1990); Gerald A. Arbuckle, *Earthing the Gospel: An Inculturation Handbook for the Pastoral Worker* (Maryknoll, New York: Orbis Books, 1990); Anthony Gittins, *Gifts and Strangers: Meeting the Challenge of Inculturation* (New York: Paulist Press, 1989); and A. A. Roest-Crollius, "What is New About Inculturation," in *Gregorianum,* vol. 59, no. 4. (1978), pp. 721–738.

10. John Paul II, *Redemptoris missio,* no. 24.

11. Vatican Council II, "Pastoral Constitution on the Church in the Modern

World," no. 58; and "Decree on the Missionary Activity of the Church," no. 22. For this and subsequent conciliar references, see Austin Flannery, ed., *Vatican II; The Conciliar and Post Conciliar Documents* (Dublin: Dominican Publications, 1977).

12. Vatican II, "Pastoral Constitution on the Church in the Modern World," no. 58.

13. Vatican II, "Decree on the Missionary Activity of the Church," no. 10, emphasis added and sentence restructured for conciseness. See also John Paul II, *Redemptoris missio,* nos. 25, 52–54.

14. Raimundo Panikkar, *Myth, Faith and Hermeneutics: Cross–Cultural Studies* (New York: Paulist Press, 1979), p. 325.

15. See Karl Rahner, "On the Theology of the Incarnation," *Theological Investigations,* 4, pp. 116–117.

16. See John Paul II, *Redemptoris missio,* nos. 5, 8, 10, 20, 28, 29.

17. Karl Rahner, "Anonymous Christianity and the Missionary Task of the Church," *Theological Investigations* 12, trans. David Bourke (London: Longman, Darton and Todd, 1974), p.176.

18. Joseph Ratzinger, *Christian Brotherhood* (London: Sheed and Ward, 1966), p. 80.

19. John Paul II, *Redemptoris missio,* nos. 8, 9, 18.

20. Bernard Lonergan, *Method in Theology* (New York: Herder and Herder, 1972), p. 247.

21. See Wolfhart Pannenberg, *Basic Questions in Theology: Collected Essays II,* trans. George H. Kehm (Philadelphia: Fortress Press, 1971), pp. 86–87. For more on syncretism, see Robert J. Schreiter, *Constructing Local Theologies* (Maryknoll, New York: Orbis Books, 1985), pp. 145–158; Lamin Sanneh, Translating the Message, pp. 22–28, 36–48; Arthur Darby Nock, *Early Gentile Christianity and Its Hellenistic Background* (New York and London: Harper and Row, Torchbooks, 1964); Paul Henry, "Hellenism and Christianity," in K. Rahner, C. Ernst, K. Smyth, eds., *Sacramentum Mundi* 3 (London: Burns and Oates; New York: Herder and Herder, 1969), pp. 10–16. See also Michael Slusser, "Diversity, Communion and Catholicity in the Early Church," *Catholic Theological Society of America: Proceedings of 45th Annual Convention* (Louisville, KY: CTSA, 1990), pp. 1–14. We are reminded here that early Christianity's expansion did not always entail the imposition of the dominant Mediterranean culture.

22. Frances Young, "Traditional Religious Cultures and the Christian Response—II, in *The Expository Times,* vol. 95 (1984), pp. 268–269: "Western secularization is surely at least partly the result of banishing religion from the stuff of daily life, and that is the result of Christianity's success in exploiting the critique of religion, particularly in its austere and rationalizing Protestant form."

23. Lizette Larson-Miller, "Christmas Season," in Peter E. Fink, ed., *The New Dictionary of Sacramental Worship* (Collegeville, Minnesota: Michael Glazier and the Liturgical Press, 1990), p.207; see also p. 205; and Brian O. McDermott, "Christ, Feasts of," in Fink, *The New Dictionary of Sacramental Worship,* p 202.

24. Bernard Lonergan, "The Dehellenization of Dogma," in *Theological Studies,* vol. 28, no. 1 (March 1967), p. 347.

25. Lonergan, pp. 123–124, 300–302.

26. Wilfred Cantwell Smith, *The Faith of Other Men* (New York: Harper and Row, 1978), p. 130.

27. Pope Nicholas V, as quoted in Peter Schineller, *op.cit.,* p. 34

28. The adaptation and translation method of these Jesuit missionaries, although less than incarnational, may be characterized as culture-sensitive, dialogical and accommodating. For more on this see Stephen Neill, *A History of Christian Missions* (Harmondsworth: Penguin Books, 1964), pp. 162–165, 183–187; and Jacques Gernet, *China and the Christian Impact: A Conflict of Cultures,* trans. Janet Lloyd (Cambridge, England, and New York: Cambridge University Press, 1985).

29. Karl Rahner, "Towards a Fundamental Theological Interpretation of Vatican II," in *Theological Studies,* vol. 40, No. 4, (December 1978), p. 717. For a slightly different translation, see the same article in Rahner's *Theological Investigations,* 20 (New York: Crossroad Publishing Co., 1981), p. 78.

30. Schreiter, *op. cit.,* p. 150.

31. Secretariat for Non-Christians, *Meeting the African Religions,* by Henri Gravrand, with a preface by Cardinal Marella (Rome: Libreria Editrice Ancora, 1968). See also Eugene Hillman, *Many Paths: A Catholic Approach to Religious Pluralism* (Maryknoll, New York: Orbis Books, 1989), pp. 46–50, 74–77, 79–80; Secretariat for Non-Christians, "The Attitude of the Church Toward the Followers of Other Religions: Reflections and Orientations on Dialogue and Mission," in *Bulletin: Secretariatus pro Non-Christianis,* 56 (1984) XIX, 2; reprint in *International Bulletin of Missionary Research,* vol. 9, no. 4 (October 1985), pp. 187–199; *Idem,* "Dialogue and Proclamation: Joint Document by the Pontifical Council for Interreligious Dialogue and the Congregation for the Evangelization of Peoples," in *Catholic International,* vol. 2, no. 17 (1–14 October 1991), pp. 805–823.

32. Francis Arinze and M. L. Fitzgerald, "Pastoral Attention to African Traditional Religion: Letter from Secretariat for Non- Christians," (25/3/1988), in *African Ecclesial Review,* vol 30, no. 3 (June 1988), pp. 131–124.

33. Maurice Otunga, "African Culture and Life-Centered Catechesis," *African Ecclesial Review,* vol. 20, no. l, Special Issue (February 1978), p. 27.

34. Bishops of Eastern Africa, "Report on the Experiences of the Church in the Work of Evangelization in Africa," in *African Ecclesial Review,* vol. 17, no. 1 (January 1975), p. 43.

35. *Idem,* "Statement of the Bishops of Africa," *African Ecclesial Review,* vol. 17, no. 1 (January 1975), pp. 56-58.

36. Asian bishops, as quoted by Bede McGregor, "Commentary on *Evangelii Nuntiandi,*" in *Doctrine and Life,* Special Issue (March/April, 1977), p. 65.

37. See Eugene Hillman, *The Roman Catholic Apostolate to Nomadic Peoples in Kenya: An Examination and Evaluation* (Maryknoll, New York: Orbis Books; Brussels: Pro Mundi Vita, 1980).

38. Karl Rahner, "Towards a Fundamental Theological Interpretation of Vatican II," in *Theological Studies,* 40, no. 4 (1979) pp. 717–718; also in *Theological Investigations* 20, trans. Edward Quinn (London: Darton, Longman and Todd, 1981), pp. 78–79.

39. Pedro Arrupe, "Catechesis and Inculturation," *Teaching All Nations,* vol. 15, no. 1 (1978), p. 21.

40. *Ibid.*

41. Peter L. Berger, *The Social Reality of Religion* (Harmondsworth: Penguin University Books, 1973), pp.29-33, 36.

42. Avery Dulles, *The Survival Of Dogma: Faith, Authority, and Dogma in a Changing World* (New York: Doubleday Image Books, 1973), p. 154.

43. See Eugene Hillman, "Religous Ethnocentrism," in *America,* (March 23, 1991), pp. 317–319.

44. Paul VI, "Evangelization in Africa Today", September 26, 1975, in *Christ to the World,* vol. 21, no. 5 (1976), p. 294; also in *L'Osservatore Romano* (October 9, 1975).

45. Evan M. Zuesse, "The Degeneration Paradigm in the Western Study of World Religions," *Journal of Ecumenical Studies,* vol. 13, no. 1 (Winter 1976), p. 21; see also p. 17: "Precisely in the area of religion we are the most subject to what may be termed 'deep'paradigms (applying Chomsky's deep structures' terminology): models of reality which pervasively shape our perceptions into a 'grammar' applying not only to ourselves but also to other selves and other possible universes as well."

46. *Ibid.,* p. 21.

47. Robert J. Schreiter, *op. cit.,* pp. 147-151.

48. E. Elochukwu Uzukwu, "Igbo World and Ultimate Reality and Meaning," in *Lucerna* (Enugu, Nigeria), vol. 4, no. 1 (January–June, 1983), p. 21.

49. *Ibid.,* pp. 21–22.

50. For more on this dualism of cultural systems, see Schreiter, *op. cit.,* pp. 148, 155.

3. AN AFRICAN TRADITIONAL RELIGION (MAASAI)

1. E. E. Evans-Pritchard, *Theories of Primitive Religion* (Oxford University Press, 1965), pp. 2–3.

2. Eboussi Boulaga, *Christianity Without Fetishes: An African Critique and Recapture of Christianity,* trans. Robert R. Barr (Maryknoll, New York: Orbis Books, 1984), p. 27.

3. Aside from my own first-hand observations and inquiries during more than two decades of living among the pastoral Maasai people in both Tanzania and Kenya, the principle sources for this chapter are listed below. But a special note of gratitude is due to Frans Mol for carefully checking my use of Maasai words; also for the facilities afforded me at the Lemek Maasai Centre, which he directs, in Narok District, Kenya.

While there are some other Maa speaking ethnic-culture groups in Kenya and in Tanzania, the so-called "agricultural Maasai," I have chosen to focus specifically upon the pastoral Maasai; and this, on the assumption that their religious traditions are more pristine, or less modified in the course of history by alien cultural influences; also because I am less familiar with the others.

4. Frans Mol, "The Meaning and Concept in Maa of 'Enkai,' (God)," in *AMECEA Apostolate to Nomads,* No. 50 (Nairobi: November 20, 1981), p. 3; Doug Priest, Jr., *Doing Theology with the Maasai* (Pasadena: William Carey Library, 1990), p. 114. On the biblical notion of God as originator, see Walter Kasper, *The God of Jesus Christ,* trans. Matthew J. O'Connell (New York: Crossroad, 1984), pp. 144–145: "The New Testament interprets the word God, which in itself is ambiguous, by the word Father. God is thus defined as the originating but himself unoriginated source of all reality....The Father alone is regarded as the unoriginated origin (*arche*) of all reality, the *principium sine principio.*"

5. Giles Pedenzini, *Samburu Prayer: A Religious Experience in Living Words,* unpublished M.A. thesis in anthropology, (Washington, DC: Catholic University of America, 1978), pp. 82- 121; Mary Phyllis Nkoitoi, *From Tribal Tradition to the Gospel of Christ: A Study of the Impact of Christianity on the Maasai of Kenya,* unpublished M.A. thesis (Rome: Gregorian University, 1973), pp. 5–10; Jan Voshaar, *Tracing God's Walking Stick in Maa: A Study of Maasai Society, Culture and Religion,* unpublished "doktorale scriptie" (Nijmegen: Catholic University of Nijmegen, 1979), pp. 127–129.

6. Frans Mol, *Maa: A Dictionary of Maasai Language and Folklore* (Nairobi: Marketing and Publishing Ltd., 1978), p. 102; Pedenzini, op. cit., pp. 74–75.

7. Mol, *Maa: A Dictionary,* p. 29; Peter Rigby, *Persistent Pastoralists: Nomadic Societies in Transition* (London: Zed Books, Ltd., 1985), p. 121, n. 11.

8. Pedenzini, *op. cit.,* p. 171.

9. *Ibid.,* p. 76; Voshaar, *op. cit.,* p. 129; Mol, "The Meaning and Concept in Maa of 'Enkai'(God)," p. 2.

10. Priest, *op. cit.,* pp. 115–116. See also Frans Mol, "The Relationship Between God and Colour Among the Maasai," *AMECEA Apostolate to Nomads,* no. 88 (March 4, 1985), pp. 1–4.

11. Pedenzini, *op. cit.,* p. 75.

12. See Monica Wilson, *Religion and the Transformation of Society: A Study in Social Change in Africa* (Cambridge: Cambridge University Press, 1971), p. 52.

13. Mol, *Maa: A Dictionary,* p. 171; Claude Hollis, The Masai: *Their Language and Folklore* (Oxford: Clarendon Press, 1905), p. 243, n. 29.

14. Paul Spencer, *The Samburu: A Study of Gerontocracy in a Nomadic Tribe* (London: Routledge and Kegan Paul, 1965), *passim.* For a similar status of senior elders in a remotely related ethnic-culture group, see also Bruno Novelli, *Aspects of Karimojong Ethnosocialogy* (Kampala and Verona: Museum Combonianum, 1988), p.48.

15. Voshaar, *op. cit.,* p. 174: *erisio Ilmaasai o Enkai.*

16. *Ibid.,* p. 175: *aingoru enkitoo.* As Frans Mol pointed out to me, *enkitoo* means "might" or "power"; *en* is a feminine prefix; *kitok* means "important," and *enkitok* is the usual word for "woman."

17. *Ibid.,* pp. 178–179. These are just some samples of the many and varied invocations used in a blessing rite and recorded by Voshaar.

18. *Ibid.*

19. Mol, *Maa: A Dictionary,* p. 134.

20. Paul Spencer, *The Maasai of Matapato: A Study of Ritual of Rebellion* (London: Manchester University Press for the International African Institute, 1988), p. 140. The attitude of the Maasai toward animals and the natural environment is noteworthy. These are generally treated with extraordinary respect. Domestic bovine animals are given individual names, they are spoken to and songs are sung about them. To kill a cat or a donkey is a serious sin (*ngok*). Even wild animals are normaly tolerated and killed only in emergency situations, when they are a threat to the people, or for food in times of famine. The traditional husbandry has established and maintained a healthy ecological balance which has been upset only as a consequence of outside forces, such as colonialism, the alienation of dry season grazing lands, subsistence and cash cropping by non-Maasai settlers in marginal rainfall areas.

21. Voshaar, *op. cit.,* p. 211.

22. John G. Galaty, "Ceremony and Society: The Poetics of Maasai Ritual," in *Man* (N.S.), vol. 18 (nd), p. 367. See also, *idem, In the Pastoral Image: The Dialectic of Maasai Identity,* Ph.D. dissertation (Chicago: University of Chicago, 1977), 425 pp.

23. Michael Maisolai ole Seraa, interviews in Ilkerin-Loita and Lemek, Narok District, Kenya (December 1990). Other informants indicated different mortuary positions, but I did not find the reason for the differences.

24. Frans Mol, personal correspondence and conversations with the author (1991).

25. Voshaar, *op. cit.,* pp. 226-227.

26 Spencer, *The Maasai of Matapato,* pp. 138-140.

27. Mol, *Maa: A Dictionary,* p. 139; Priest, *op. cit.,* p. 112.

28. Spencer, *The Maasai of Matapato,* pp. 141-142.

29. Clifford Geertz, *The Interpretation of Cultures* (New York: Basic Books and Harper Torchbooks, 1973), p. 30; Hans Küng et al., *Christianity and the World Religions: Paths of Dialogue with Islam, Hinduism and Buddhism* (New York: Doubleday, 1989), p. xvi.

30. Peter L. Berger, *The Social Reality of Religion* (Harmondsworth: Penguin Books, 1967), pp. 33, 48.

31. Spencer, *The Maasai of Matapato,* pp. 42–43, 47.

32. *Ibid.,* p. 200. For more on fertility rites, see Priest, *op. cit.,* pp. 194–203.

33. Victor W. Turner, *The Ritual Process: Structure and Anti- Structure* (Chicago: Aldine Publishing Co., 1969), pp. 52–53.

34. Spencer, *The Maasai of Matapato,* p. 221.

35. Galaty, *In the Pastoral Image,* p. 312.

36. *Ibid.,* pp. 297 ff.

37. Mol, *Maa: A Dictionary,* pp. 103–104, 141.

38. Priest cites one example of a prophetess/healer calling the people back to

their traditional values, and warning them against the destructive ways of modernity: *op. cit.,* p. 194–195.

39. Robert N. Bellah, "Religious Evolution," in Ronald Robertson, ed., *Sociology of Religion* (Harmondsworth: Penguin Books, 1969), p. 263; from *American Sociological Review,* Vol. 29.

40. David Tracy, *The Analogical Imagination: Christian Theology and the Culture of Pluralism* (New York: Crossroad, 1981), p. 383.

41. Gregory Baum, *Religion and Alienation: A Theological Reading of Sociology* (New York: Paulist Press, 1975), p. 146.

4. POSSIBLE APPLICATIONS

1. Bernard Lonergan, *Method in Theology* (New York: Herder and Herder, 1972), pp. 300, 362–363.

2. John Paul II, *Redemptoris missio,* no. 24.

3. Paul VI, *Evangelii nuntiandi,* no. 63.

4. John Paul II, *Redemptoris missio,* no. 55.

5. Avery Dulles, *Models of the Church* (Garden City, New York: Doubleday Image Books, 1978), p. 24.

6. Ibid., p. 25; *Idem, The Survival of Dogma: Faith, Authority and Dogma in a Changing World* (Garden City, New York: Doubleday Image Books, 1973), pp. 15, 25.

7. George B. Wilson, "Don't Blame the Liturgists," *America,* vol. 165, no. 16 (Nov. 23, 1991), p. 384.

8. This paragraph owes much to Bernard Cooke, *The Distancing of God: the Ambiguity of Symbol in History and Theology* (Minneapolis, Fortress Press, 1990), pp. 356–359, 366–367.

9. Avery Dulles, *The Survival of Dogma,* p. 26.

10. William M. Thompson, *The Jesus Debate: A Survey and Synthesis* (New York: Paulist Press, 1985), p. 349. See also Francis Schussler Fiorenza, "Redemption," in Komonchak, Collins and Lane, eds., *The New Dictionary of Theology* (Collegeville, Minnesota: Liturgical Press and Michael Glazier, 1987), p. 842.

11. Dulles, *The Survival of Dogma.,* p. 184. See also Roger Haight, "Salvation in Liberation Theology," in The Ecumenist, vol. 26. no. 2 (January–February, 1988), p. 17.

12. Bernard Lonergan, *op. cit.,* p. 302.

13. *Ibid.,* pp. 300–302.

14. Robert J. Schreiter, *Constructing Local Theologies* (Maryknoll, New York: Orbis Books, 1985), pp. 150–151.

15. For more on inculturation relative to marriage as structured by most of Africa's peoples, see Eugene Hillman, *Polygamy Reconsidered: African Plural*

Marriage and the Christian Churches (Maryknoll, New York: Orbis Books, 1975).

16. Karl Rahner, "Basic Theological Interpretation of the Second Vatican Council," *Theological Investigations* 20, trans. Edward Quinn (London: Darton, Longman and Todd, 1981), p. 79.

17. For more on inculturation through interreligious dialogue, see Eugene Hillman, *Many Paths: A Catholic Approach to Religious Pluralism* (Maryknoll, New York: Orbis Books, 1989).

18. Karl Rahner, *Meditations on Freedom and the Spirit* (London: Burns and Oates, 1977), p. 11; see also pp. 19–29. See also David Hollenbach, *Justice, Peace and Human Rights* (New York: Crossroad, 1987), pp.224–225.

19. Vatican II, "Pastoral Constitution on the Church in the Modern World," no. 62.

20. Vatican II, "Decree on the Missionary Activity of the Church," no. 22.

21. Maurice Otunga, "African Culture and Life-Centered Catechesis," *African Ecclesial Review,* vol. 20, no. 1 (February 1978), p. 28.

22. Karl Rahner, "Basic Theological Interpretation of the Second Vatican Council," p. 86.

23. For documentation on the acceptance of slavery by the Catholic bishops of the United States on the eve of the War between the States, and its acceptance by the Vatican's Holy Office even after that war, see E. Hillman, *Polygamy Reconsidered,* pp. 184–185, 211–212.

24. See Bernard Cooke, *The Distancing of God,* pp. 348–347, 356–357, 359.

25. See D. R. Jones, "Sacrifice and Holiness," in S. W. Sykes, ed., *Sacrifice and Redemption* (New York: Cambridge University Press, 1991), p. 12 and 17, where the author speaks of "what was Canaanite and legitimately baptized into the biblical system," and what was repudiated, noting also that "Jesus drew on elements which were part of the complex of the Old Testament and in Judaism as a whole."

26. See Hans Küng, *The Church* (New York: Sheed and Ward, 1967), p. 110: "When the Jewish passover meal—Jesus' Last Supper was in all probability a passover meal—ceased to be important for the Gentile Christians, there remained this eschatological meal of the community, which Paul was then to see more profoundly as 'the Lord's Supper.'"

27. Gerald A. Arbuckle, *Earthing the Gospel: An Inculturation Handbook for the Pastoral Worker* (Maryknoll, New York: Orbis Books, 1990), pp. 101–102.

28. Robert J. Daly, "Sacrifice," in Peter E. Fink, ed., *The New Dictionary of Sacramental Worship* (Dublin: Gill and Macmillan, 1990), p. 1137.

29. Albert Nolan, *Jesus Before Christianity: the Gospel of Liberation* (London: Darton, Longman and Todd, 1977), p. 73.

30. John M. Huels, "Interpreting Canon Law in Diverse Cultures," in *The Jurist,* vol. 47 (1989), p. 260.

31. See *Ibid.,* for views and references on the matter of the eucharistic meal, pp. 281–284. For the views of distinguished African theologians, see Eugene Uzukwu, "Food and Drink in Africa and the Christian Eucharist," in *African Ecclesial Review* vol. 22, no. 6 (December 1980), pp. 370–385; and Jean-Marc Ela, *African Cry,* trans.

Robert R. Barr (Maryknoll, N.Y.: Orbis Books, 1986), pp. 3–7.

32. For a preliminary inquiry, see Doug Priest Jr., *Doing Theology with the Maasai* (Pasadena: William Carey Library, 1990), pp. 133–170, 178–180.

33. On the various meanings of "sacrifice," see Robert J. Daly, *The Origin of the Christian Doctrine of Sacrifice* (London: Darton, Longman and Todd, 1978), *passim;* also Michael F. C. Bourdillon and Meyer Fortes, eds., *Sacrifice* (New York and London: Academic Press, 1980), *passim.*

34. Edward Hulmes, "The Semantics of Sacrifice," in Sykes, *Sacrifice and Redemption,* p. 266.

35. See Priest, *op. cit.,* pp. 30–35, 180–192.

36. See Hans Küng, *op. cit.,* pp. 107–110: "The fellowship of Jesus' disciples even after Pentecost appeared to be no more than a religious party within the Jewish nation: 'the sect of the Nazarenes' (Acts 24:5; cf. 24:14; 28:22). They were a kind of separate synagogue....They met in the temple (Acts 2:46), apparently approved Jewish sacrificial customs (cf. Mt 5:23 f.) and the paying of the temple tax (cf. Mt. 17:24–27) and apparently submitting themselves to the judgment of the synagogues (cf. Mk 13:9; Mt 10:17)....They seem to have complied fully with the Old Testament law (Mt 5:17–19)....Can we not assume that the first disciples of Jesus were fully and entirely members of the people of Israel, whose religious and legal practice marks a continuation of their life as part of the Jewish nation?...."

37. Wilson, "Don't Balame the Liturgists," p. 385.

38. John Paul II, *Redemptoris missio,* no. 52.

39. *Ibid.,* no. 24, emphasis added.

40. See Amos N. Wilder, "Myth and Dream in Christian Scripture," in Joseph Campbell, ed., *Myths, Dreams and Religion* (New York: E. P. Dutton, 1970; Dallas: Spring Publications, 1988), pp. 75–79. See also Wolfhart Pannenberg, *Basic Questions in Theology: Collected Essays II,* trans. George H. Kehm (Philadelphia: Fortress Press, 1971), pp. 86–87: "This religion (Christianity) not only linked itself to Greek philosophy, but also inherited the entire religious tradition of the Mediterranean world—a process whose details have still not been sufficiently clarified, but which was probably decisive for the persuasive power of Christianity in the ancient world."

41. *Diognetus,* 5:1-2-4-5, trans. Eugene Fairweather, in Cyril C. Richardson, ed., *Early Christian Fathers* (New York: Macmillan, 1970), pp. 216–217; as quoted by Michael Slusser, "Diversity, Communion and Catholicity in the Early Church," in *Catholic Theological Society of America: Proceedings of 45th Annual Convention* (Louisville: CTSA, 1990), p. 2.

Index